P9-CSV-826

More Advance Praise for **Sway**

"Extremely thoughtful and intelligent."
— *Miami Herald*

"*Sway* is a reminder that we are, without a doubt, the most complicated, confounding, and conflicted life form on earth . . . *Sway* begins to shed some much-needed light on the forces that can drive anyone, be it your customers, your coworkers, your boss, or your spouse, beyond rational or logical thought."
—Scott Bedbury, former Chief Marketing Officer for Starbucks and Worldwide Advertising Director for Nike, and author of *A New Brand World: 8 Principles for Achieving Brand Leadership in the 21st Century*

"If you think you know how you think, you'd better think again! Take this insightful, delightful trip to the sweet spot where economics, psychology, and sociology converge, and you'll discover how our all-too-human minds actually work."
—Alan M. Webber, founding editor of *Fast Company* magazine

"As frightening as it is fascinating, *Sway* is a quick, compelling read that will have a lasting impact on all your future decisions."
—Rory Freedman, coauthor of the #1 *New York Times* bestseller *Skinny Bitch*

"A breathtaking book that will challenge your every thought, *Sway* hovers above the intersection of *Blink* and *Freakonomics.*"

—Tom Rath, coauthor of the *New York Times* #1 bestseller *How Full Is Your Bucket?*

"Now we know why no one ever coined the phrase 'rational exuberance.' Behind the surprising ways we all make choices, the Brafmans find biology, humanity, and the wisdom of our collective experience. As a longtime student of how financial decisions are made, I found their insights utterly fascinating. Once I started reading, I couldn't stop—and I suspect the Brafmans could tell you exactly why!"

—Sallie Krawcheck, CEO, Citi Global Wealth Management

"Count me swayed—but in this instance by the pull of entirely rational forces. Ori and Rom Brafman have done a terrific job of illuminating deep-seated tendencies that skew our behavior in ways that can range from silly to deadly. We'd be fools not to learn what they have to teach us."

—Robert B. Cialdini, author of the *New York Times* bestseller *Influence*

"Brilliant."

—Klaus Schwab, chairman of the World Economic Forum

"*Sway* helped me recognize an aspect of irrational behavior in my experimental work in physics. Sometimes I have jumped into some research that didn't feel quite right . . . but some irrational lure, such as the hope of quick success, pulled me in."

—Martin L. Perl, 1995 Nobel Laureate in Physics

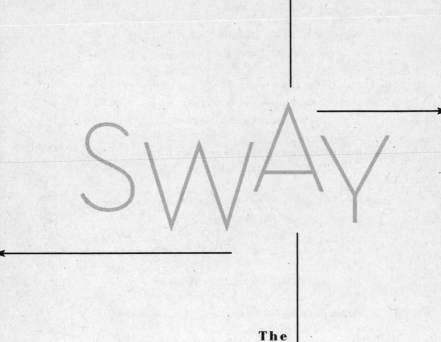

SWAY

The
Irresistible
Pull
of
Irrational
Behavior

ORI BRAFMAN AND ROM BRAFMAN

BROADWAY

Copyright © 2008 by Ori Brafman and Rom Brafman

All Rights Reserved

Published in the United States by Broadway Books, an imprint of The Crown
Publishing Group, a division of Random House, Inc., New York.
www.crownpublishing.com

A hardcover edition of this book was originally published in 2008 by
Doubleday.

BROADWAY BOOKS and the Broadway Books colophon are trademarks
of Random House, Inc.

All trademarks are the property of their respective companies.

Book design by Chris Welch

Library of Congress Cataloging-in-Publication Data
Brafman, Ori.
Sway : the irresistible pull of irrational behavior / Ori Brafman and
Rom Brafman.
p.   cm.
Includes bibliographical references and index.
1. Rationalism—Psychological aspects. 2. Irrationalism (Philosophy)
3. Stupidity. 4. Errors. 5. Conduct of life. 6. Success. I. Brafman, Rom.
II. Title.
BF441.B725 2008
155.9'2—dc22
2007045640
ISBN: 978-0-385-53060-6

PRINTED IN THE UNITED STATES OF AMERICA

7 9 10 8

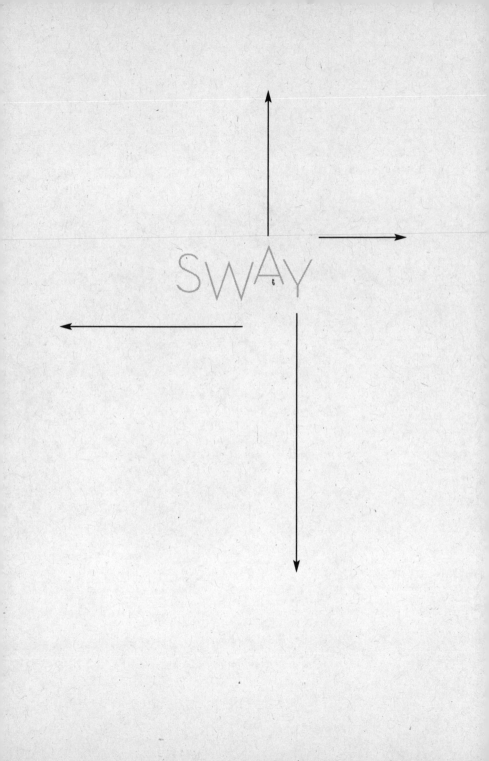

Broadway Books

New York

TO NIRA,

FOR ALWAYS BELIEVING IN US

Contents

Preface 1

A little house on the Tel Aviv prairie. Asbestos and open-heart surgery. Ignoring the O-ring. Diagnosing the wrong patient. Where psychology and business collide.

↓

Chapter One

ANATOMY of an ACCIDENT 9

Taking off at Tenerife. The oversensitive egg shoppers. The lure of the flat rate. Would you like insurance with that? So long, Martha's Vineyard.

Contents

Chapter Two

The SWAMP of COMMITMENT 25

Playing not to lose. Fun-n-Gun. Only the Gators walked out
alive. The $204 twenty-dollar bill. The end of the Great Society.
"We don't even know where the tunnel is."

↓

Chapter Three

The HOBBIT and the MISSING LINK 41

The real-life Indiana Jones. The hunt for the missing link.
The Stradivarius on the subway. What's in a five-cent hot dog,
anyway? Homer Simpson and Piltdown Man. Can a discount
drink decrease IQ? Shakespeare was wrong.
A paleontological lineup.

↓

Chapter Four

MICHAEL JORDAN and the FIRST-DATE INTERVIEW 65

The curse of the low draft pick. The "cold" professor. What
lovesick college freshmen have in common with HR managers.
When a pretty face equals a higher interest rate. The "mirror,
mirror" effect. The Joe Friday solution.

↓

Chapter Five

The BIPOLAR EPIDEMIC and the CHAMELEON EFFECT 89

A psychiatric outbreak. Sugar pills and Prozac. Tricking Israeli
army commanders. How to sound beautiful. How old
do you feel? The love bridge.

Contents

Chapter Six

In FRANCE, the SUN REVOLVES AROUND the EARTH   111

Who wants to trick a millionaire? Splitting the pie. Sentimental
car dealers. The talking cure for felons and venture capitalists.
Russian justice. The rational Machiguenga.

Chapter Seven

COMPENSATION and COCAINE   131

Switzerland's toxic conundrum. The GMAT rebels. The power
of the pleasure center. Hijacking altruism. Fast times at
"Commie High." The anticipation factor.

Chapter Eight

DISSENTING JUSTICE   149

The Supreme Court conference. Peer pressure and Coke-bottle
glasses. Ferris Bueller and the blocker. "We are not focusing
on the name you give to potatoes." The captain is not God.
Not just thinking out loud. Justice has been served.

Epilogue   169

Swimming with the riptide. The power of the long view.
Zen economics. Propositional thinking. One man's trash is
one woman's masterpiece. A cable guy, a banker, and
a pharmaceutical rep. The real devil's advocate.

Acknowledgments   183
Notes   187
Index   201

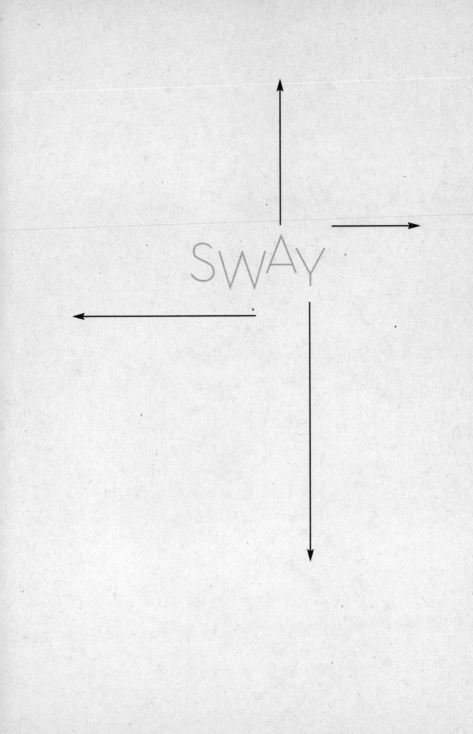

Preface

A little house on the Tel Aviv prairie.

Asbestos and open-heart surgery.

Ignoring the O-ring.

Diagnosing the wrong patient.

Where psychology and business collide.

When we were growing up, our mother had two idols she hoped we would try to emulate. The first—and there was really no competition there—was Laura Ingalls of *Little House on the Prairie* fame. In our mom's eyes, she was the picture of perfection. We'd talk back to our mom, and she'd sternly ask, "Would Laura Ingalls ever talk that way?" We'd forget to do our homework, leave dirty dishes in the sink, or generally cause trouble, and Laura Ingalls would travel from the nineteenth-century American prairie to 1980s Tel Aviv and admonish us to get with the program.

The second heroic figure was our mom's cousin Reli, a hotshot lawyer who was valedictorian at Harvard Law. In our eyes, too, Reli could walk on water.

Although Ori thought about law school when he was in

eleventh grade, neither one of us took up a legal career. But if you count Reli in, we form the Jewish mother's equivalent of the holy trinity: Reli, the lawyer; Rom, the psychologist (we'll call him a doctor); and Ori, the businessman.

In a way, this book was born from our different paths in life. While Rom was completing his PhD in psychology, Ori was getting his MBA. On day one of business school, expecting to find himself immersed in a sea of finance, economics, and accounting, Ori realized in his first class, with Professor Roberto Fernandez, that this would be no tranquil sea. Fernandez had a voice that could project from here to the moon. He had that larger-than-life aura about him that made you sit on the edge of your seat. "I have some news for you," he told the class of eager MBA students that first day. "People aren't rational." And with that, Fernandez turned on a grainy film, shot in the 1950s, of open-heart surgery. "See that white stuff they're pouring over the guy's heart?" Fernandez narrated. "It's asbestos." People gasped, unsure of how to react.

"I'm serious," he boomed. "Unsurprisingly, the patients administered the asbestos started dying off." But the hospital had continued with the procedure. How often, Fernandez asked the class, do we turn a blind eye to objective information?

Then he shifted gears and passed around copies of a table featuring mechanical engineering data about a synthetic rubber seal called an O-ring. "Take a look at this chart," he said. "It represents the likelihood of a mechanical failure as temperatures drop." The data showed that at around 32°F, the O-ring would lose its pliability and malfunction. None of the students knew where this was going.

It turned out that the O-ring in question was part of the design of the Space Shuttle *Challenger*. The night before the launch, engineers from the company that had built the O-ring recommended that the launch be delayed because they did not have conclusive proof that it would hold up in the cold weather predicted for the next day. Despite their concerns, however, management decided to proceed with the launch.

As Ori's class listened, mesmerized, Fernandez launched into similar stories of irrational behavior: movie executives bullied into hiring an actress who was obviously wrong for the part, a manufacturer that knowingly produced airplane brakes that caught fire, and more.

Fernandez's point was that although most of us think of ourselves as rational, we're much more prone to irrational behavior than we realize. It was a point that stayed with Ori long after business school, and it made us realize that our future professions had a lot more in common than we might originally have thought. Fernandez became a regular part of our vocabulary. Referring to someone who was obviously acting irrationally, we'd say: "This is a total Fernandez situation." And we found such situations everywhere we looked: in our own lives, in stories we read about the missteps of Fortune 500 companies, and in the actions of politicians.

Meanwhile, while we never quite lived up to the Laura Ingalls standard, as fate would have it, we did both become writers. The true genesis for this book came after a dinner conversation Ori had with a doctor who had been practicing obstetrics for the better part of thirty years. Dr. Jenkins possessed all the qualities you'd hope for in an OB/GYN—he was patient, he listened, he was smart, and most of all, he was experienced. You could count on him to make the right decision.

The conversation drifted to group dynamics and how emotions play a major role in decision making. Without thinking, Ori said, "I'm sure it's very different in your profession, where you're all scientists."

The doctor's face took on a serious expression as he explained that doctors are by no means immune to irrational forces. And because lives are on the line, the repercussions of irrational behavior can be devastating.

Take what happened to ER doctor Brian Hastings, who shared a story of how irrational behavior can derail even the most professional of physicians.

A few weeks earlier a woman had arrived at the emergency room in a panic. Her two-year-old daughter, Amy, she said, was experiencing severe stomach pains. Abdominal pains might signal a condition as benign as indigestion, but the woman was worried it might be something more serious. Normally, doctors would start running tests and evaluating Amy's symptoms.

Dr. Hastings paused in his story and quickly enumerated a litany of procedures the ER physicians could have performed. Rather than focusing on Amy, however, the doctors focused their attention on her mother: she was flustered and anxious and appeared overly concerned—basically, she seemed to be the type of parent who'd overreact. The physicians made a judgment call to send Amy home.

The very next day Amy and her mom were back in the emergency room. Physicians know that when treating toddlers it's absolutely vital to listen to their parents, who usually have an acute sense of when something is wrong with their child. But at the same time, the doctors now had even more evidence that Amy's mom was overreacting: here she was again at the hospital, showing all the signs that she was the kind of hypochondriac they refer to as a "frequent flyer." Once more the doctors sent Amy home without running any tests.

The third day started out pretty much the same way as the previous two. Amy and her mother returned; the doctors became even more convinced that the mother was overreacting. It was only when Amy lost consciousness that the doctors realized something was terribly wrong. But by then it was too late. Dr. Hastings shook his head as he recalled, "We lost her."

Had they considered the situation fully, the ER doctors would have recognized the need to keep Amy under observation. But instead they ignored the warning signs and repeatedly sent the toddler home. The moment the physicians labeled Amy's mom a "frequent flyer," they fell under the spell of an irrational force we call the *diagnosis bias*—in other words, the moment we label a person or a situation, we put on blinders to all evidence that contradicts our diagnosis.

Why would these skilled and experienced physicians make a choice that contradicted their years of training and ultimately cost the life of a child? We wanted to understand what was going on in this situation and the countless others in which people are swayed from the logical path.

What psychological forces underlie our own irrational behaviors? How do these forces creep up on us? When are we most vulnerable to them? How do they affect our careers? How do they shape our business and personal relationships? When do they put our finances, or even our lives, at risk? And why don't we realize when we're getting swayed?

In this book we'll explore several of the psychological forces that derail rational thinking. Wherever we looked— across different sectors, countries, and cultures—we saw different people being swayed in very similar ways. We're all susceptible to the sway of irrational behaviors. But by better understanding the seductive pull of these forces, we'll be less likely to fall victim to them in the future.

Chapter ¹

ANATOMY of an ACCIDENT

Taking off at Tenerife.

↓↓↓↓

The oversensitive egg shoppers.

↓↓↓

The lure of the flat rate.

↓↓

Would you like insurance with that?

↓

So long, Martha's Vineyard.

The passengers aboard KLM Flight 4805 didn't know it, but they were in the hands of one of the most experienced and accomplished pilots in the world. Captain Jacob Van Zanten didn't just have a knack for flying. His attention to detail, methodical approach, and spotless record made him a natural choice to head KLM's safety program. It was no surprise, then, that the airline was keen to show him off. One magazine ad featuring the smiling captain captured it all: "KLM: from the people who made punctuality possible." Even seasoned pilots—not exactly the type of individuals prone to swoon—regarded him as something of a celebrity.

On the flight deck of the 747, en route from Amsterdam to Las Palmas Airport in the Canary Islands, Van Zanten must have felt a sense of pride. Today's trip was moving along with the smooth precision that had become his hallmark. The schedule was straightforward: land in Las Palmas, refuel, and transport a new set of passengers back home to Holland.

But then Van Zanten got an urgent message from air-traffic control. A terrorist bomb had exploded at the airport flower shop, causing massive chaos on the ground; Las Palmas would be closed until further notice.

The captain knew that at times like this the most important thing was to remain calm and proceed with caution. He had performed drills preparing for this kind of situation countless times. In fact, Van Zanten had just returned from leading a six-month safety course on how to react in exactly this kind of situation.

Following standard procedure, the captain obeyed orders to land fifty nautical miles from his original destination, on the island of Tenerife. There, at 1:10 p.m., his plane joined several others that had been similarly diverted.

Now, you don't need to be a seasoned airline pilot to appreciate that Tenerife was no JFK. It was a tiny airport, with a single runway not meant to support jumbo jets.

With his plane safely parked at the edge of the runway, the captain checked his watch. Seeing the time, he was struck with a worrisome thought: the mandated rest period.

The Dutch government had recently instituted strict, complicated rules to which every pilot had to adhere. After getting in touch with HQ and performing some quick calculations, Van Zanten figured the latest he could take off was 6:30 p.m.

Flying after the start of his mandated rest period was out of the question—it wasn't just against policy; it was a crime punishable by imprisonment. But taking the rest period would open its own can of worms. Here in Tenerife there would be no replacement crew to take over. Hundreds of passengers would be stranded overnight. That would mean the airline would have to find them a place to stay, and there weren't enough hotel rooms on the island. In addition, a delay here would initiate a cascade of flight cancellations throughout KLM. A seemingly minor diversion could easily become a logistical nightmare.

It's easy to imagine the stress that Van Zanten was experiencing and why he became so determined to save time. It was like being stuck at a red light when you're late for a big meeting. Try as you might to stay calm, you know that your reputation is on the line; your frustration grows, and there's really not much you can do. But there was one thing Van Zanten *could* do: the captain decided to keep the passengers on board, so that when Las Palmas reopened, he could get back in the air immediately.

But the air-traffic control personnel who worked at Tenerife tower were of a different mind-set. Here was a small airport on a tropical island, now inundated with planes from all over the world that had been diverted because of the Las Palmas explosion. Not only was the tower understaffed, but the air-traffic controllers were in no hurry to get planes out of the gate; they were, in fact, getting ready to listen to a live soccer match on their transistor radios. Twenty minutes after landing, Van Zanten received word from the tower that he should let his passengers off: it looked like they would be here for a while.

From there, events at Tenerife continued to move forward like molasses. Twenty minutes turned into an hour. The captain spent every moment thinking of ways to minimize the delay. He held a strategy session with his crew. He called KLM headquarters to find out exactly how much time he had left before the mandated rest period kicked in. An hour on the ground had turned into two; then the captain came up with another idea. He decided to refuel at Tenerife and thus shave half an hour off the turnaround in Las Palmas.

But this time-saving idea backfired. As soon as Van Zanten started refueling, word came from Las Palmas that the airport had finally reopened. But it was too late to stop the thirty-five-minute refueling process.

Finally, just when it looked like the plane was set to go, nature threw its own wrench into the plan: a thick layer of fog descended upon the runway.

Kicking himself over his decision to refuel, Van Zanten became even more intent on getting under way. With the fog growing thicker, visibility dropped to just 300 meters—so poor that gazing out the cockpit window the captain couldn't see the end of the runway.

Van Zanten knew that every moment the fog got worse made it that much likelier that the Tenerife tower would

shut down the airport. He saw that his window of opportunity to get out of Tenerife before an overnight stay was
closing. It was now or never—time to go.

But what the captain did next was completely out of character. Van Zanten revved up the engines, and the plane
lurched down the runway.

"Wait a minute," Van Zanten's copilot said in confusion.
"We don't have ATC clearance."

"I know that," replied the captain as he hit the brakes.
"Go ahead and ask."

The copilot got on the radio and received *airway* clearance—approval of the flight plan. But the tower said nothing about the vital *takeoff* clearance. And yet, determined to
take off, Van Zanten turned the throttles to full power and
roared down the foggy runway.

The jumbo jet was gaining momentum when, seemingly
out of nowhere, the scariest sight Van Zanten could have
imagined appeared before him. A Pan Am 747 was parked
across the runway, and Van Zanten was approaching it at
take-off speed.

There was no way to stop or swerve. Instinctively, Van
Zanten knew that his only chance was to take off early.
"Come on! Please!" the captain urged his plane. He pulled
the aircraft's nose up desperately, dragging its tail on the
ground and throwing up a blinding spray of sparks.

The nose of Van Zanten's plane managed to narrowly
clear the parked 747. But just when it looked like he was in

the clear, the underside of Van Zanten's fuselage ripped through the top of the Pan Am plane.

The KLM plane burst into a fiery explosion as it hurtled another five hundred yards down the runway.

Van Zanten, his entire crew, and all of his passengers were killed. In all, 584 people lost their lives that day.

The aeronautical community was stunned. It was by far the deadliest airplane collision in history. An international team of experts descended on Tenerife airport. They examined every bit of evidence, interviewed the eyewitnesses, and scrutinized every moment of the cockpit recorders in an attempt to pinpoint the cause of the accident.

The experts quickly ruled out a mechanical failure or terrorist attack. Piecing together the events of that day, it was clear that the other plane on the runway, Pan Am Flight 1736, had missed a taxiway turnoff and ended up in the wrong place. The thick fog contributed to the disaster. Van Zanten couldn't see the Pan Am plane, the Pan Am pilot couldn't see him, and the tower controllers couldn't see either one of them. On top of that, the tower was undermanned and the controllers were distracted by the day's events.

Despite all these factors, though, the tragedy would never have occurred if Van Zanten hadn't taken off without clearance. Why would this seasoned pilot, the *head of safety* at the airline, make such a rash and irresponsible decision?

The best explanation the investigators could come up with

was that Van Zanten was feeling frustrated. But that didn't quite add up. Feeling frustrated is one thing; completely disregarding protocol and forgetting about safety is another.

Clearly, Van Zanten was experienced. Clearly, he was well trained. And clearly, he was good at what he did. How could he cast aside every bit of training and protocol when the stakes were so high?

The aeronautical experts turned over every stone in their search for an explanation. But there was something in Tenerife that remained completely hidden. Alongside the rolling fog and crowded airfield, an unseen psychological force was at work, steering Van Zanten off the path of reason.

A growing body of research reveals that our behavior and decision making are influenced by an array of such psychological undercurrents and that they are much more powerful and pervasive than most of us realize. The interesting thing about these forces is that, like streams, they converge to become even more powerful. As we follow these streams, we notice unlikely connections among events that lie along their banks: the actions of an investor help us to better understand presidential decision making; students buying theater tickets illuminate a bitter controversy in the archeological community over human evolution; NBA draft picks point to a fatal flaw in common job-interview procedures; women talking on the phone show why a shaky bridge can be a powerful aphrodisiac.

Charting these psychological undercurrents and their unexpected effects, we can see where the currents are strongest and how their dynamics help us understand some of the most perplexing human mysteries. These hidden currents and forces include loss aversion (our tendency to go to great lengths to avoid possible losses), value attribution (our inclination to imbue a person or thing with certain qualities based on initial perceived value), and the diagnosis bias (our blindness to all evidence that contradicts our initial assessment of a person or situation). When we understand how these and a host of other mysterious forces operate, one thing becomes certain: whether we're a head of state or a college football coach, a love-struck student or a venture capitalist, we're all susceptible to the irresistible pull of irrational behavior. And as we gain insight about irrational motives that affect our work and personal lives, fascinating patterns emerge, connecting seemingly unrelated events.

Let's examine the first of these streams, to help us solve the mystery of what happened with Captain Van Zanten. We find our first clue in an unlikely place—the egg and orange juice aisles of our neighborhood supermarket.

Professor Daniel Putler, a former researcher at the U.S. Department of Agriculture, has spent more time thinking about eggs in a year than the rest of us spend in a lifetime. He carefully tracked and studied every aspect of egg sales in southern California. Looking at the data, he found some interesting patterns. Egg sales, for instance, were typically higher during the first week of each month. Not surprisingly, they were abnormally high in the weeks leading up to Easter, only to experience a sharp decline the week after.

That was all well and good, but Putler's next discovery wasn't just of use to the USDA and Al the grocer. Poring over cash-register data that reflected egg-price fluctuations, Putler identified what is referred to in economics as an "asymmetry."

Now, *traditional* economic theory holds that people should react to price fluctuations with equal intensity whether the price moves up or down. If the price goes down a bit, we buy a little more. If the price goes up a bit, we buy a little less. In other words, economists wouldn't expect people to be more sensitive to price increases than to price decreases. But what Putler found was that shoppers completely overreacted when prices rose.

It turns out that, when it comes to price increases, egg buyers are a sensitive bunch. If you reduce the price of eggs, consumers buy a little more. But when the price of eggs rises, they cut back their consumption by *two and a half times.*

Anyone who's made a shopping list with a budget in mind can tell you how this plays out. If the price drops, we're mildly pleased. But if we see that the price has gone up since last week, we get an *oh no* feeling in the pit of our stomachs and decide it's cereal for breakfast that week instead of scrambled eggs. This feeling of dread over a price increase is disproportionate—or asymmetric—to the satisfaction we feel when we get a good deal.

We experience the pain associated with a loss much more vividly than we do the joy of experiencing a gain. Sensing a loss as a result of the high price, the shoppers can't help but put the carton back on the shelf.

And it's not only egg buyers who are affected by the pain of a loss. A group of researchers replicated Putler's study among orange juice shoppers in Indiana and arrived at the exact same results: Midwest OJ drinkers are just as finicky about price increases as are Los Angeles omelet makers. Regardless of geography and breakfast preferences, losses loom larger than gains.

Putler's research illuminates a mystery that economists have been grappling with for years. For no apparent logical reason, we overreact to perceived losses.

This principle is key to understanding Van Zanten's actions. But before we return to Tenerife and the investigation, it's important to see how our aversion to loss plays out in our own decision making.

Think about the seemingly straightforward decision we make when we sign up for a new phone service. After wading through the phone company's electronic menus, we're presented with a choice: we can either pay for service by the minute or opt for a flat monthly fee and talk till the cows come home. Chances are that the pay-as-you-go plan is our better bet. Most of us just don't talk enough to justify a flat-rate plan.

But at this point loss aversion kicks in; we start imagining ourselves gabbing like teenagers into the night. The fear of a monstrous bill looms, and we sign up for the unlimited plan "just in case."

Economists can scold us for making a poor choice, but in deciding which service to sign up for, we're willing to sacrifice a little bit to avoid a potential loss.

AOL stumbled upon this same phenomenon when, after years of charging clients by the minute for their dial-up Internet access, it introduced a flat-billing option. The results were catastrophic, but not in the way you'd think. As AOL's CEO explained, the flat-pricing plan was "working too well." New customers were signing up in droves, and for three months AOL's servers were completely jammed. As with the phone service, Internet users wanted to avoid the perceived loss associated with pay-as-you-go.

The word *loss* alone, in fact, elicits a surprisingly powerful reaction in us. Companies like Avis and Hertz, facing the challenge of selling a product that is both useless and overpriced, have capitalized on this powerful effect. When we rent cars, our credit cards—not to mention our own car insurance—automatically cover us should anything go wrong with the vehicle. But the rental companies push additional coverage that not only is redundant but would cost a whopping $5,000 on an annual basis. Normally, we'd scoff at such a waste of money. But then, as the sales rep behind the counter is about to hand over the keys to that newish Ford Taurus, he asks whether we'd like to buy the *loss damage* waiver.

When we hear those words, our minds begin to whir: What if I have bad luck and end up in a wreck? What if, for some reason, my credit card won't cover me after all? Normally, we'd never dream of taking out an extra policy at an astronomical rate just to be doubly safe, but the threat of a loss makes us reconsider.

Looking at the larger picture, the behavior of the supermarket shoppers, phone customers, Internet subscribers, and car renters is strikingly similar to that of Captain Van Zanten. The losses that Van Zanten was trying to avoid were all the downsides of the mandated rest period: the cost of putting up the passengers, the chain reaction of delayed flights, and the blot on his reputation for being on time.

Van Zanten's desire to avoid a delay started out small enough. At first he simply wanted to keep the passengers on board to save time. But as the delay grew longer, the potential loss loomed larger. By the time an overnight delay seemed almost inevitable, Van Zanten was so focused on avoiding it that he tuned out all other considerations and, for that matter, his common sense and years of training.

Of course, there's a big difference between signing up for a phone service and causing the tragedy at Tenerife. Needlessly spending a few dollars is one thing; taking off without tower clearance is another. You would think that in such a situation, with hundreds of lives on the line, the captain would have exercised greater caution and acted even more deliberately than he would have under normal circumstances. That brings us to our second clue. As Columbia Business School professor Eric Johnson explained to us, the more meaningful a potential loss is, the more loss averse we become. In other words, the more there is on the line, the easier it is to get swept into an irrational decision.

If anyone knows about having a lot on the line, it's Jordan Walters of the Silicon Valley branch of the investment house Smith Barney. Jordan is exactly the kind of person you'd look for in a financial planner: he's calm, he's thoughtful, and he always takes the time to listen. As we sat down in his office and sipped from the minibar-sized can of apple juice he'd offered us, it was easy to forget that just outside the door associates were calling in millions of dollars in stock trades.

The thing about Jordan is that he isn't just a numbers guy. He genuinely cares about his clients, and when they make bad decisions, it bothers him. He remembers one client in particular. "A fellow comes in," Jordan recalled. "He had a business he'd started, a biotech start-up that got bought over by a public company—and he's made! They were going to retire! In Martha's Vineyard!"

That "fellow" was clearly on a high. He'd probably told everyone—from the gardener to his kids' teacher to his old college buddies—about his windfall.

But Jordan pointed out to his new client that investing the vast majority of his wealth in his biotech company stock would be putting all his eggs in one basket: "Oh my gosh, it's such a big concentration—we need to find a way to wean ourselves out of this." It would have made a lot more sense to diversify, and Jordan came up with a solid plan: Sell a predetermined percentage of your holdings every quarter, he advised his client, "so you take the emotion out of the decision."

But the investor wanted to ride the stock even higher. He had just sold his company. He'd made it big. Why stop now? "Well, what happened," Jordan recalled, "when he came in and the stock was at $47, we sold maybe 10 percent of his total position."

Shortly after that, the stock began to drop. "The stock was down to $42 and he says, 'If the stock goes back to $47, I'm going to sell.'"

Sensing that money was starting to slip through his fingers, the client developed an aversion to loss that was strikingly similar to Van Zanten's. Like the captain who was preoccupied with getting back on schedule, the investor was blindly focused on getting back to even.

Jordan realized that his client was so eager to make up for a loss that he was becoming oblivious to the risks he was taking. "What about the downside?" he asked the client. Now, from Jordan's rational perspective, there was nothing magical about the $47 stock price, and there was no guarantee that the stock would get back up there. On the flip side, the stock was liable to slip even further. But for the client, selling at anything less than $47 represented a loss—a bogeyman to be avoided at all costs.

"Well, the stock goes down to $38," Jordan recalled, "and the investor says, 'You know what, if it goes back to $44, I'll sell it then.'" Stock traders call this kind of behavior "chasing a loss"—when investors ignore the current data, put on blinders, and proceed with singular purpose to recover as much of their loss as possible.

Jordan explained to his client that holding on to the position in hopes that the stock price would recover was much too risky. But the client would have none of it, and took matters into his own hands. He ignored Jordan's advice and kept his stake. "[The stock] ended up at twelve cents," Jordan said. "The only thing he got out of that, the only value, was the initial 10 percent [he sold up front]."

Painful as it might have been, the investor could have sold at $42, perhaps giving up the dream of the fancy yacht but keeping the majority of his assets and realizing his plan to retire to Martha's Vineyard. Likewise, Van Zanten could have accepted the small blot on his reputation for punctuality and spent the night at Tenerife. Surely it wasn't worth it for either man to risk everything—be it a huge nest egg or the lives of his passengers—just to avoid a potential loss. You'd think that with a great deal on the line, people would play it safe. But, as Jordan explained, "You may not see that the stock is going to go into a tailspin. I would say you may misinterpret it." That's when this hidden force takes over.

So now we have two important clues. First, Van Zanten overreacted to a potential loss. Second, because so much was on the line, he was even more susceptible to taking a dangerous risk. But there's another missing clue. In order to get to the bottom of the Tenerife mystery, we'll need to visit the Swamp.

Chapter 2

The SWAMP of COMMITMENT

Playing not to lose.

Fun-n-Gun.

Only the Gators walked out alive.

The $204 twenty-dollar bill.

The end of the Great Society.

"We don't even know where the tunnel is."

Kayaking on the University of Florida's Lake Wauburg can be a disconcerting experience. The scene is quintessentially southern. The lake, or should we say swamp, is surrounded by wild marsh grass and a canopy of towering trees draped in thick Spanish moss, their roots dipping into the warm water. Insects buzz day and night, and the mosquitoes can drive you mad.

The romance quickly fades away, though, when you see a pair of reptilian eyes staring up at you from the water. True to the school's mascot, the lake is full of alligators. It's said that they don't attack adults, but, paddling along in a plastic kayak, you're not so sure.

Lake Wauburg is home to many an alligator, but it's not the most notorious swamp in Gainesville. That honor goes to

UF's football stadium, affectionately dubbed "the Swamp." Each fall an army of campers, RVs, and SUVs descends upon the campus, and grown men walk around clutching stuffed alligators as game time approaches.

Amidst all this hubbub, with the excitement of an upcoming game in the air, lies the final missing piece of the Van Zanten puzzle.

Even in the chaos of a campus gearing up for a Gators game, Steve Spurrier felt right at home. He grew up in the South and played for Florida as a star quarterback, winning the coveted Heisman Trophy. Twenty-three years later, he returned to UF's football stadium to coach the team.

The most flattering way to describe the Gator team upon Spurrier's arrival in 1990 was as a "fixer-upper." The team had never won a conference title; in fact, it was on probation because of allegations of rule violations by the team's former coach.

To say that Spurrier had a job on his hands is an understatement. Against all odds, though, the coach led a turnaround so dramatic that it still lives on in the memory of fans years later. Spurrier's charisma, his rapport with his team, and the new player talent he brought in all helped put the Swamp on the map. But Spurrier's most important move was to identify a weak spot in the strategy employed by his opponents.

For years the teams in the conference had adhered to a "war of attrition" game strategy: they called conservative plays and held on to the ball for as long as they could, hoping to win a defensive battle. The idea wasn't necessarily to score a lot of points. It was to wear down the opponent and eat up time. In other words, the coaches were playing not to lose.

When you think about it, the conference coaches were acting a lot like Jordan Walters's investor who lost his windfall from the biotech company: rather than focusing on maximizing their gains, they concentrated on avoiding losses. It was exactly this mentality that opened a window of opportunity for Spurrier. In the simplest terms, Spurrier came to dominate the conference by playing to win, by introducing what he called the "Fun-n-Gun" approach.

When we caught up with Spurrier, he explained that, like all coaches, he had his list of conservative plays: "You know, like little screen passes, little short passes behind the line. You got a chance to have a surefire completion." But Spurrier also mixed things up with a generous helping of "big chance plays, where you got to give your players a shot." In other words, Spurrier's team passed more often, played more aggressively, and tried to score more touchdowns.

The Fun-n-Gun strategy took the Southeast conference by storm. UF's stadium earned its nickname, "the Swamp," because "only Gators," it was said, "walked out alive."

And here's where the first of our two hidden forces or sways comes into play. Spurrier gained an advantage because the other coaches were focused on trying to avoid a potential loss. Think of what it's like to be a college football coach. As you walk around town, passing fans offer themselves up as instant experts on the game—never afraid to give you a piece of their minds on what you did wrong in yesterday's match-up. You make one bad move and you get skewered by fans and commentators alike. Meanwhile, ticket sale revenues, your school's alumni fund-raising, and your job all depend heavily on the football team's success. All of that pressure adds up. Just as with Putler's egg shoppers, the losses loom large. As Coach Spurrier explained to us, "What coaches start thinking is, don't do anything to lose the game."

You'd have thought that after losing a few games to a team like the University of Florida Gators—much less having a losing season—the coaches would have reevaluated their war-of-attrition model.

But they didn't.

And so Spurrier and his Gators continued to dominate former powerhouses like Alabama, Tennessee, and Auburn. Over the next six years, the coach and his team went on to win four division titles, culminating in the national championship. All the while, opposing coaches continued to stick with the old model.

The coaches fell victim not only to loss aversion, but also to another closely linked sway called *commitment*. In other words, they had used the grind-it-out-and-hold-on-to-the-ball strategy for so long that it was simply hard for them to let go. They were committed to continuing down the road they had always walked. They were so committed, in fact, that it was virtually impossible for them to take a different path. Trying to avoid potential losses led the coaches to adopt a war-of-attrition model, and commitment to what they'd been doing for years made them unable to react to Spurrier's superior strategy.

We've all experienced the pervasive pull of commitment in some form or another; whether we've invested our time and money in a particular project or poured our energy into a doomed relationship, it's difficult to let go even when things clearly aren't working. As difficult as it can be to admit defeat, however, staying the course simply because of a past commitment hurts us in the long run.

Independently, each of these two forces—commitment and aversion to loss—has a powerful effect on us. But when the two forces combine, it becomes that much harder to break free and do something different.

It's precisely because of the compounding effect of these two forces that students in Max Bazerman's negotiations class at Harvard Business School would do well to hold on to their wallets when he introduces his "twenty-dollar auction." They say it's easy to take candy from a baby; Professor Bazerman has found that it's just as easy to take money from Harvard MBAs.

On the first day of class, Professor Bazerman announces a game that seems innocuous enough. Waving a twenty-dollar bill in the air, he offers it up for auction.

Everybody is free to bid; there are only two rules. The first is that bids are to be made in $1 increments. The second rule is a little trickier. The winner of the auction, of course, wins the bill. But the runner-up must still honor his or her bid, while receiving nothing in return. In other words, this is a situation where second best finishes last.

Indeed, at the beginning of the auction, as people sniff out an opportunity to get a $20 bill for a bargain, the hands quickly shoot up, and the auction is officially under way. A flurry of bids follows. As Bazerman described it, "The pattern is always the same. The bidding starts out fast and furious until it reaches the $12 to $16 range."

At this point, it becomes clear to each of the participants that he or she isn't the only one with the brilliant idea of winning the twenty bucks for cheap. There is a collective hard swallow. As if sensing the floodwaters rising, the students get jittery. "Everyone except the two highest bidders drops out of the auction," Bazerman explained.

Without realizing it, the two students with the highest bids get locked in. "One bidder has bid $16 and the other has bid $17," Bazerman said. "The $16 bidder must either bid $18 or suffer a $16 loss." Up to this point the students were looking to make a quick dollar; now neither one wants to be the sucker who paid good money for nothing. This is when the students adopt the equivalent of football's war-of-attrition model. They become committed to the strategy of playing not to lose.

Like a runaway train, the auction continues, with the bidding going up past $18, $19, and $20. As the price climbs higher, the other students don't know whether to watch or cover their eyes. "Of course," reflected Bazerman, "the rest of the group roars with laughter when the bidding goes over $20."

From a rational perspective, the obvious decision would be for the bidders to accept their losses and stop the auction before it spins even further out of control. But that's easier said than done. Students are pulled by both the momentum of the auction and the looming loss if they back down—a loss that is growing greater by the bid. The two forces, in turn, feed off each other: commitment to a chosen path inspires additional bids, driving the price up, making the potential loss loom even larger.

And so students continue bidding: $21, $22, $23, $50, $100, up to a record $204. Over the years that Bazerman has conducted the experiment, he has never lost a penny (he donates all proceeds to charity). Regardless of who the bidders have been—college students or business executives attending a seminar—they are always swayed.

The deeper the hole they dig themselves into, the more they continue to dig.

We've already seen how Captain Van Zanten was affected by the power of loss aversion: it was incredibly important for him to avoid the mandated rest period. But add to that the force of commitment and you have a situation that could sway even the most experienced and capable of professionals.

By the time Van Zanten reached the end of the foggy runway, the pain of his potential losses seemed so massive—and he had already committed himself so firmly to getting off the island—that in his mind he could not seriously entertain any plan other than taking off.

This same compounding effect of loss aversion and commitment repeats itself time and again—even in the highest echelons of American government.

If 1950s politics was like an episode of *Survivor*, LBJ was surely the hands-down winner.

It's hard to find an instance when LBJ wasn't being strategic. There's a thin line between determination and intimidation, and LBJ had no trouble skipping between the two. When he was elected to Congress, he'd call fellow legislators at all hours of the night, just to catch them off guard. Later, as president, during official White House meetings he'd shock and intimidate visitors by announcing a swimming break, taking off his clothes, and jumping naked into the pool.

But he didn't employ these tactics for kicks alone. LBJ had a cause that was close to his heart. While other politicians hailed from a world of privilege, LBJ had grown up surrounded by poverty. He had seen firsthand just how difficult life could be for poor people in the South.

"Some men," LBJ once said, "want power simply to strut around the world and to hear the tune of 'Hail to the Chief.' Others want it simply to build prestige, to collect antiques, and to buy pretty things. Well, I wanted power to give things to people—all sorts of things to all sorts of people." Specifically,

LBJ was dedicated to easing the plight of the poor and giving African-Americans and other minorities the rights they deserved.

He made it his mission to complete the work started by FDR during the Depression. Johnson admired the social progress that had been achieved through the New Deal but felt that FDR's ultimate goal of realizing social change was still unfinished.

LBJ used his bulldog strategies to launch the most important campaign of his career: the war on poverty. Towering over others at six foot three, he would literally get in people's faces, encroach on their personal space, and bulldoze allies and enemies alike into submission. With the passing of the Civil Rights Acts, the establishment of antipoverty community programs, and the launch of Medicare, Medicaid, and federal education funding, the "Great Society"—one of the biggest social reform programs in American history—took shape.

In 1964 LBJ was at the height of his political prowess. America had begun to recover from the JFK assassination. Congress was heavily Democratic, Johnson's approval ratings were sky-high, and most legislators were either sympathetic to his cause or too intimidated to oppose him. "I knew Congress," he later reflected, "as well as I knew Lady Bird."

But just as his lifelong dream of enacting massive reform—from making urban ghettos a thing of the past to providing universal health care—was beginning to materialize, LBJ unknowingly became a participant in Bazerman's auction.

There are three essential elements to the auction. There's the $2 phase—where with wide-eyed optimism everyone's banking on winning the equivalent of a free lunch. And there's the final phase—where participants are bidding upward of $20, digging themselves deeper into a hole, but are unwilling to let go. But the most interesting phase is the middle stage, at $12 to $16, when it first becomes clear where the train is heading. And it's here that loss aversion and commitment meet.

LBJ entered his auction in much the same way that Bazerman's students did. But instead of a $20 bill, the prize dangled in front of him was the opportunity to stop the spread of communism in Southeast Asia.

To the president, the North Vietnamese communists seemed like weak opponents. They lacked a powerful army, sophisticated technology, money, and broad international support. LBJ cast his first bid—the equivalent of $2—by launching an aerial bombing campaign in 1965 aimed at eroding support for the communists. With the United States fighting against a less powerful enemy and with a massive arsenal at its disposal, things looked promising—as is always the case in the first stage of the Bazerman auction.

But just a few years later LBJ was already deep into the third stage of the auction. With more than 500,000 troops on the ground in 1968 and tens of thousands dead, LBJ was long past the $20 mark. He lamented, "Light at the end of the tunnel, hell, we don't even have a tunnel; we don't even know where the tunnel is." Like the coaches in Spurrier's conference, the president was getting beat but could not bring himself to change course.

In the end, Johnson lost more than just Vietnam. The war cost him the full realization of the Great Society, his approval ratings, and ultimately—when he decided not to run for another presidential term—his political career. Many years later he reflected, "I knew from the start that I was bound to be crucified either way I moved." He explained, "If I left the woman I really loved—the Great Society—in order to get involved with that bitch of a war on the other side of the world, then I would lose everything at home. All my programs . . . all my dreams to provide education and medical care . . ." But he also recognized, "If I left that war and let the Communists take over South Vietnam . . . there would follow in this country an endless national debate—a mean and destructive debate—that would shatter my presidency, kill my administration, and damage our democracy."

Ironically, that's exactly what happened anyway. But it is what went on at the second stage of the auction—the $12–$16 phase—that is the key to understanding how Johnson was swayed in his decision making. On the one hand, LBJ could see where the war was headed. A phone conversation the president had with his national security advisor in May of 1964 is incredibly telling. "I just stayed awake last night thinking of this thing," LBJ confided. "The more that

I think of it I don't know what in the hell, it looks like to me that we're getting into another Korea. It just worries the hell out of me. I don't see what we can ever hope to get out of there with once we're committed . . . I don't think it's worth fighting for and I don't think we can get out. And it's just the biggest damn mess that I ever saw."

But on the other hand, just a few moments later LBJ acknowledged his fear that "if you start running from the Communists, they may just chase you right into your own kitchen."

Driven forward by the momentum of the "auction" and the dread of capitulating to a loss, LBJ abandoned the possibility of retreat. And that's what happens in the $12–$16 stage. Oddly enough, the convergence of the two undercurrents brings about exuberant optimism. When looking a potential loss in the face, we hope against hope that everything will turn out okay.

In fact, if you listen more closely to LBJ's speeches, the exuberance, the determination, and, for that matter, the entire approach start to sound eerily familiar. LBJ's message, and even the specific words he used to describe Vietnam, bear an uncanny resemblance to George W. Bush's remarks about Iraq.

"There is no easy answer, no instant solution," declared LBJ. "There is no magic formula for success in Iraq," proclaimed Bush.

These similarities in thinking aren't the product of shared personality or political ideology but rather of a common dialect; both men are using the language of the Bazerman auction.

Both presidents showed strong commitment and resolve to stay the course. LBJ stated, "We will not be defeated. We will not grow tired. We will not withdraw, either openly or under the cloak of a meaningless agreement." President Bush asserted, "We will not fail. We will persevere and defeat this enemy and hold this hard-won ground for the realm of liberty."

And then there's the optimism. As the Vietnam situation grew increasingly out of control, LBJ declared, "There has been substantial progress, I think, in building a durable government during these last three years." Similarly, when it became evident that the Iraq war wasn't going to result in an easy victory, Bush boasted, "Iraq has a new currency, the first battalion of a new army, representative local governments, and a Governing Council with an aggressive timetable for national sovereignty. This is substantial progress."

Nobel Prize–winning economist Daniel Kahneman, who, together with Amos Tversky, first discovered and chronicled the phenomenon of loss aversion, offers a telling reflection of our psychology during such situations. "To withdraw now is to accept a sure loss," he writes about digging oneself deeper into a political hole, "and that option is deeply unattractive." When you combine this with the force of commitment, "the option of hanging on will therefore be relatively attractive, even if the chances of success are small and the cost of delaying failure is high."

Aversion to loss, on its own, is strong. But when it converges with commitment, the force becomes an even more powerful influence in shaping our thinking and decision making.

As we'll soon see, commitment is often bolstered by yet another force, one that will take us on the ultimate quest: the search for the missing link.

Chapter 3

The HOBBIT and the MISSING LINK

The real-life Indiana Jones.

The hunt for the missing link.

The Stradivarius on the subway.

What's in a five-cent hot dog, anyway?

Homer Simpson and Piltdown Man.

Can a discount drink decrease IQ?

Shakespeare was wrong.

A paleontological lineup.

t was one of those moments you see in the movies—just add the Indiana Jones theme music to complete the picture. In the fall of 2004 Dr. Dean Falk, an anthropology professor and forensic expert, was sitting at home next to her computer. When the phone rang, the first thought that crossed her mind was, "I hope it's not a telemarketer." She never imagined how much that call was about to change her life.

"Hi," said the man on the other end of the line. "My name is David Hamlin, and I'm with the National Geographic Society." As if reading her mind, he quickly added, "I'm not selling magazines."

Hamlin could barely contain his excitement. "I've been dying to talk with you for at least two months. I haven't been able to because what I'm about to tell you was embargoed until right now; but the embargo just lifted, so now I'm free to talk about it."

"Are you putting me on? Is this real?" Falk asked.

Hamlin laughed. "I can assure you it is. I just returned from Indonesia, where we filmed for National Geographic television," he said. "I'm calling you because Mike Morwood, the discoverer, recommended you."

Hamlin started to tell Falk about an unexpected find made by Morwood, at the time a little-known Australian anthropologist, on the remote island of Flores in the Java Sea.

The interesting thing about Flores and islands like it, Falk later explained to us, is that when it comes to evolution, they are great equalizers. Small species grow larger, and large ones become smaller—converging, more or less, at the size of a German shepherd. Nobody knows exactly why this island-effect phenomenon occurs, but scientists speculate that it's a result of genetic adaptation to an environment with relatively few predators and a limited supply of resources. Indeed, over the decades anthropologists working in Flores have discovered bone remains that could have belonged to creatures from *Alice in Wonderland*: from six-foot-long lizards to giant rats to dwarf elephants.

But also amidst these bones were found sophisticated stone tools, some dating back hundreds of thousands of years, tools that—it was thought—could have been made only by humans. The catch, though, was that humans hadn't arrived on the island until forty thousand years ago. "There are no hominids for a long, long time," Falk explained to us, "just tools." Someone had to have fashioned those artifacts, someone possessing both intelligence and manual dexterity. Yet there was no archeological evidence to indicate who that someone might have been.

This is where Morwood's discovery comes in—a discovery that was, anthropologically speaking, mind-boggling. The finding purported not only to solve the mystery of the sophisticated tools, but also to shed new light on a branch of our evolution.

Falk didn't suspect that along with a significant discovery she was about to encounter a psychological undercurrent that had swayed the anthropological community a century earlier. Not only does this force regularly alter our perceptions of other people and our experiences, it caused hundreds of people to ignore a violin prodigy giving a free concert, imbued an energy drink with the power to alter students' IQs, and played a role in the biggest fraud in scientific history.

Although she didn't know it yet, Falk was about to witness history repeating itself. Back in the 1850s, the scientific world was in the midst of a revolution. When bone remains of an ancient hominid were found in Germany's Neander Valley, scientists struggled to make sense of what this creature could have been. Its features closely resembled ours, but something about the skeleton was not quite human. It had a more pronounced nose, a thicker skull, and a squatter body shape—in other words, it looked like what we now think of when we imagine a caveman. At first the scientists figured that the remains belonged to a Russian soldier who had met an untimely death in the Napoleonic Wars. But Darwin's *Origin of Species* cast things in a whole new light. When viewing the remains through the lens of evolutionary theory, the scientists surmised that they must have belonged to a recent ancestor of modern humans—an entirely new species we know today as Neanderthal.

At the time, evolution was believed to be a linear progression (whereas the modern theory sees evolution as resembling a much more complex family tree). Following this logic, scientists felt there was an obvious gap in the progression from apes to the more humanlike Neanderthals. This "missing link" became a holy grail for European scientists.

But you can't go searching for a missing link without having *some* idea of what you're looking for. The scientists developed the equivalent of a police sketch of this mysterious creature: they figured it would have a big brain but the physical appearance of an ape. With that, they started digging.

During that same time, a precocious young Dutch student named Eugene Dubois was becoming fascinated with evolution. Indeed, later in life Dubois would make one of the most important finds of all time—one that would have surprising implications for Dean Falk and the Flores discovery in the twenty-first century.

By the time Dubois was twenty-nine, he had earned his degree in medicine (finishing at the head of his class), gotten married, had a baby daughter, and taken on a university professorship. Over the years the scientists in Europe had continued to dig, but they had little more than piles of rocks to show for their efforts. The missing link remained elusive.

After spending months reviewing all the literature and theories on the subject, Eugene Dubois concluded that the scientists were looking in all the wrong places. He decided to quit his professional career and move his young family to the East Indies, where many prehistoric ape remains had been found over the years. There, Dubois was certain, the missing link was waiting to be discovered.

Since he had minimal funding, no government backing, and no organizational support, life for Dubois and his family was anything but easy. Dubois came down with malaria, and he and his wife lost a newborn child to tropical disease. The work was grueling—exploring dense, uncharted territory, descending into unexplored caves, even confronting tigers. But three years into the search Dubois hit gold. In October 1891, his team was exploring in a region called Ngawi, colloquially known as the "hellhole of Java." The place was hot, desolate, and known for ancient lava eruptions.

The day seemed like any other until the team happened upon what at first looked like a coconut shell. A closer look revealed something much more spectacular. It was a skull. "Near the place on the left bank of the river . . . ," Dubois reported, "a beautiful skull vault has been excavated." The skull was certainly not that of an ape: "As far as the species is concerned, the skull can be distinguished from the living chimpanzees: first because it is larger, second because of its higher vault."

Near this find Dubois discovered a leg bone that clearly belonged with the skull. But the femur looked like it had been severely injured, as if struck by an arrowhead, and subsequently healed. This was significant because it showed that the individual must have been cared for and treated by her community—untended, the injury would have immobilized her and she wouldn't have lived to see the bone heal.

Dubois knew he was onto something momentous. All the pieces pointed to one conclusion: a new prehistoric species, more advanced than apes but not quite human. And this evolutionary link was a lot more like us than anyone had imagined. She even walked upright. "It is obvious from the entire construction of the femur," Dubois wrote, "that this bone fulfilled the same mechanical role as in the human body." The only major difference was the structure of the skull and its size, which was smaller than that of modern humans. Rather than having a big brain and apelike physique, the missing link turned out to have a humanlike body and a smaller brain.

Dubois was elated with the find. He documented all the facts, drew comprehensive sketches, and carefully verified his results. But the reaction Dubois received from the scientific community was not what he expected. One expert took issue with the skull size and dubbed the finding a modern victim of microcephaly (a neurological disorder that causes reduced brain size) "of an unusually elongated type." Another thought the fossil was that of a "giant gibbon of some kind." Yet another insisted that the skull and femur were completely unrelated. Dubois tried to defend his find, but for years the discovery remained largely ignored.

When we look at this story in light of what we've learned about commitment, it's easy to understand why the scientists dismissed Dubois. The anthropologists at that time were committed to a certain view of evolution. A hominid with a small brain who walked on two legs and belonged to a community simply didn't fit this view. It was much easier to dismiss Dubois's find as an abnormal human or a strange gibbon than to change their theory of human evolution.

Still, Dubois was perplexed and offended. He prided himself on being a man of science, and he expected other scientists to respect his rigorous methodology. After all, he had carefully documented every aspect of the dig and included elaborate sketches of his find. But the fossil of what we know today as *Homo erectus*—one of the most momentous discoveries in anthropological history—remained stashed in Dubois's house for decades.

The way in which the scientists responded to Dubois in the nineteenth century is critical for us to understand, because it sheds light on the next force we'll encounter. While a part of their dismissive reaction can be explained by their commitment to a previously held belief, there was also another force at play. Here's where commitment merges with the sway of "value attribution": our tendency to imbue someone or something with certain qualities based on perceived value, rather than on objective data.

To understand how value attribution works and how it swayed the anthropological community, we'll need to fast-forward to the present day and journey beneath the streets of Washington, D.C. On a January morning in 2007, L'Enfant Plaza subway station was about to be filled with music. At exactly 7:51 a.m., during rush hour, an ordinary-looking man dressed in jeans and wearing a baseball cap nonchalantly took out his $3.5 million Stradivarius violin and got ready to play. The man was Joshua Bell, one of the finest violinists alive, who regularly performs to sold-out crowds in the best concert halls. Unbeknownst to any of the commuters, Bell was taking part in an undercover field study conducted by the *Washington Post.*

Bell's subway performance started with Bach's Sonatas and Partitas for Unaccompanied Violin, one of the most challenging pieces ever composed for the instrument. Over the next forty-three minutes the concert continued, but on that January morning there was no thunderous applause. There were no cameras flashing. Here was one of the best musicians in the world playing in the subway station for free, but no one seemed to care. Of the 1,097 people who walked by, hardly anyone stopped. One man listened for a few minutes, a couple of kids stared, and one woman, who happened to recognize the violinist, gaped in disbelief.

Now, the commuters might have been in too much of a hurry to pay attention to Bell. But clearly, had there been news cameras present, or had people known this man was a virtuoso, at least a *few* more people would have stopped to listen. But think about how Joshua Bell appeared to the subway riders. He wasn't dressed in formal attire; he stood on no stage. For all intents and purposes, Bell looked like your average, run-of-the-mill street performer. Even though he didn't *sound* like a mediocre violinist, he looked the part. Without realizing it, the commuters attributed the value they perceived—the baseball cap, the jeans, the subway venue—to the quality of the performance. As they passed by Bell, most subway riders didn't even glance in his direction. Instead of hearing an outstanding concert, they heard street music.

The D.C. commuters who dismissed Bell's performance were swayed by value attribution in the same way that anthropologists were swayed to ignore Dubois's discovery. Everything associated with the fossil of *Homo erectus* was perceived by the scientific community as having little value: Dubois, its discoverer, was a virtual no-name; the European scientists looked down their noses at the prospect of the "hellhole of Java" being home to a human ancestor; and the fossil's brain size was too small to fulfill anthropological preconceptions of what the missing link would look like. It was as if Dubois were holding a Stradivarius in his hands but no one paid attention because he was wearing a baseball cap and jeans and standing in a subway station.

It's easy to understand, though, why the scientists and subway riders reacted the way they did. Value attribution, after all, acts as a quick mental shortcut to determine what's worthy of our attention. When we encounter a new object, person, or situation, the value we assign to it shapes our further perception of it, whether it's our dismissal of a curiously inexpensive antique we find at a flea market or our admiration of a high-priced designer bag in a chic boutique. Imagine, for instance, stumbling upon a discarded armoire on the street. Do you see it for the rare treasure it might be? Or is your knee-jerk reaction that *something* must be wrong with it? In the same way, value attribution affects our perceptions of people. We may turn down a pitch or idea that is presented by the "wrong" person or blindly follow the advice of someone who is highly regarded.

That is not to say that a person's title doesn't count for anything or that a product's price doesn't often give you a good idea of its true value. But when we apply that price tag (be it real or metaphorical) too broadly, we compromise our rationality. Take what happened when Coney Island visitors encountered entrepreneur Nathan Handwerker's new food stand. When he went into business in 1916, the Polish immigrant decided to undercut the competition. Everyone else was charging ten cents for the classic Coney Island meal—the hot dog—so Handwerker priced the dogs he made from his wife's old recipe at a mere five cents. Despite the fact that Handwerker's hot dogs were every bit as delicious as the competition's (and were made from real beef), he attracted almost no customers. Visitors to Coney Island viewed these mysterious half-priced hot dogs as inferior and wondered what cheap, substandard ingredients went into the recipe. It didn't help when Handwerker offered free pickles or free root beer to hot dog buyers. Sales remained flat and, if anything, giving away freebies only further cemented the value attribution.

It wasn't until Handwerker came up with a clever new ploy that his hot dogs really started selling. He recruited doctors from a nearby hospital to stand by his shop eating his hot dogs while wearing their white coats and stethoscopes. Because people place a high value on physicians, customers figured if doctors were eating there, the food had to be good. So they soon started buying from Handwerker, and his "Nathan's Famous Hot Dogs" took off. It makes you wonder just how many times we miss out on something worthwhile because of our preconceptions about its value.

But preconceptions go both ways. As we'll see, the very phenomenon of value attribution that worked against Eugene Dubois led the same community of scientists to wholeheartedly embrace an unscrupulous charlatan. After Dubois's discovery, other hominid fossils were found throughout the world. But England had remained discovery-free—that is, until Charles Dawson came along.

Unlike Dubois, who was an unknown Dutch scientist, Dawson was British, respected, and well known and had been elected to a fellowship in the Geological Society of London. The tale he spun to his fellow scientists was this: He had been strolling along a dirt road outside of Piltdown Common in Sussex when he happened upon a piece of flint. The flint was obviously out of place, so Dawson asked some nearby ditchdiggers about it. They confirmed that they had unearthed the flint and discarded it along the dirt path. The conversation that followed supposedly went something like this:

"Say, did you happen to find any skulls in the course of your dig?"

"No."

"Well, let me know if you do."

According to Dawson, he visited the laborers every now and then, and, sure enough, during one of the visits they had something for him: a hominid skull. Over the following months, more pieces of the skull mysteriously turned up, including a remarkably well-preserved jawbone. It was with these alleged artifacts that Dawson marched into London's British Museum (Natural History). For good measure, he threw an authentic ancient elephant tooth into the mix, presumably from a prehistoric inhabitant that must have roamed the British savannah.

It's important to understand how crude Dawson's specimen (dubbed *Piltdown Man*) was. The skull had belonged to a medieval man but had been dunked in a bucket of brown paint to make it look older. The jaw had come from a modern orangutan whose teeth had been filed to make it look more or less human. You didn't need to be Sherlock Holmes to realize the specimen was a fraud.

The best way of describing the physical model that was constructed based on Piltdown Man is to note its striking resemblance to Homer Simpson. As the curator of the British

Museum (Natural History) wrote, Piltdown was "perhaps ungainly, and may have walked with a shuffling gait, but his brain and skull were essentially human, only with a few ape-like traits." Seeing the diorama of Piltdown in the British Museum, gently polishing a stick tool, you almost expect him to exclaim, "D'oh!"

But when the British scientists looked at Piltdown Man, they didn't see a crude specimen. They marveled at the new find, because it confirmed two cherished beliefs. First, Piltdown Man proved that civilization had indeed originated in England. One anthropologist boasted, "It bucks me up to think that England is coming up trumps." The scientists felt a sentimental connection with the fossil. He was seen as an ancient forefather, "indeed a man of the dawn." A pillar was erected at the site of the ditch where Dawson claimed to have found the bones. The inscription proudly announced, "Here in the old river gravel Mr. Charles Dawson, F.S.A., found the fossil skull of Piltdown."

Piltdown Man also confirmed scientists' assumption that the missing link would have a humanlike brain and apelike features.

If only Dubois's *Homo erectus* fossil had received half the fanfare. Instead, few anthropologists accepted it as authentic. Piltdown, on the other hand, was embraced by the vast majority of the scientific community. Only decades later, in 1952, did scientists finally—and cautiously—debunk the great hoax.

Why would the scientific community dismiss Dubois's authentic discovery and embrace Dawson's forgery? Once again, it comes down to value attribution. If Dubois was dressed in metaphorical baseball cap and jeans, Dawson was decked out in full concert regalia—tails and all. In other words, Dawson was perceived as distinguished and reputable and his findings were considered to be of high value. Moreover, Dawson alleged that he had found his remains on British soil, rather than in the hellhole of Java; and the Piltdown specimen's brain was large, in contrast to the relatively tiny (and apelike) skull of Dubois's find.

Now, while most of us would like to think we'd be able to tell the difference between a real fossil and a skull dipped in paint, let's put ourselves in the British scientists' shoes. Every major institution deemed Dawson's discovery genuine. The press was in a frenzy and the head of the British Museum supported the find.

Once we attribute a certain value to a person or thing, it dramatically alters our perceptions of subsequent information. This power of value attribution is so potent that it affects us even when the value is assigned completely *arbitrarily*. To see this process in action, let's visit a group of economists who set up a clever experiment using SoBe Adrenaline Rush, a beverage that claims to increase mental acuity. To test acuity, the researchers developed a thirty-minute word jumble challenge that was administered to three groups of students.

The first group, a control group, took the test without drinking any SoBe. The second group was told about the intelligence-enhancing properties of SoBe, given the drink, and asked to watch a video while the tonic had time to take effect. These students also were required to sign an authorization form allowing the researchers to charge $2.89 to their university account for the SoBe. We'll call this second group of students the "fancy-shmancy SoBe" drinkers. Finally, a third group of students was given the same spiel about SoBe but was told that the university had gotten a discount and that they would only be charged eighty-nine cents for the drink. We'll call them the "cheapo SoBe" drinkers.

Now, the results of the experiment were surprising. The group that drank the fancy-shmancy SoBe performed slightly better on the test than did the group that received no SoBe at all. But before we rush out to buy SoBe, with its acuity-enhancing powers, it's important to note that the students who drank the cheapo SoBe performed significantly worse than either the fancy-shmancy group or the SoBe-free control group. Given that exactly the same SoBe beverage was served to both groups, we can only conclude that it was the *value* the students attributed to the SoBe that made the difference in their test scores. Strange as it may sound, fancy-shmancy SoBe made the students smarter, while cheapo SoBe hindered their performance.

"The intriguing idea," Dan Ariely, one of the study's authors, told us, "is that expectations change the reality we live in." The value that we attribute to something fundamentally changes how we perceive it. "When you get something at a discount, the positive expectations don't kick in as strongly." And once we attribute a certain value to something, it's very difficult to view it in any other light.

When Joshua Bell dresses up and plays at a concert hall, he's regarded like fancy-shmancy SoBe—and his talent more than merits his audience's appreciation. But when Bell plays the same instrument and music "at a discount" at the subway station, he's perceived like cheapo SoBe. Whenever we're called upon to make judgments, value attribution plays a role, often altering our reactions to a person or thing. Who hasn't had their views about a movie shaped, even before they watched it, because they heard or read the opinions of critics? Even when it comes to our own enjoyment or entertainment, we're not immune to the powerful influence of value attribution. It turns out that Shakespeare was wrong after all: a rose by any other name really doesn't smell as sweet.

Columbus, Ohio, home of Ohio State University, isn't the kind of place where you'll find glitzy Broadway-style theater. Still, students and community members alike had long appreciated the Ohio State theater department's productions. For $15 any theater aficionado could buy a season pass and gain access to all ten shows in that semester's scheduled lineup.

Unbeknownst to the first sixty people who purchased a season pass one year, they were about to play a key role in an economic study. "After the person announced his or her intention to buy a season ticket," the study's authors explained, "the ticket seller sold the purchaser one of three types of tickets, which had been randomly ordered beforehand." One-third of them received a regular, full-priced, $15 ticket; one-third

SWAY

received a $2 discount on their tickets; the rest received their tickets at a discount of $7.

Those receiving the bargain tickets were told that the discount was being given as part of a theater department promotion. Regardless of the price of the ticket, however, all subscribers had equally good seats.

It turns out, though, that the price we pay for a ticket affects our enjoyment of the performance. Although it's difficult to measure how highly audience members value a play—we don't know how enthusiastically everyone clapped or how hard each laughed—we can track whether they return for subsequent performances.

As the researchers pointed out, given that the attendees all held the same ticket books to the ten plays in the series, from a rational economic perspective, all the theatergoers should have been equally likely to attend subsequent plays.

But those who paid full price attended significantly more shows than did those who received either the $2 or the $7 discount. One explanation is that the full-price ticket holders perceived that with each show they attended they were recouping a part of their initial investment (i.e., the price for the season pass). Thus those who had paid full price went to more shows because their investment was higher. But there was virtually no difference in attendance levels between the two discount groups. If the desire to recoup their investment were the only force at play, you'd expect that the group that received the $7 discount would skip more shows than did the group that received only a $2 discount. But this wasn't

58

the case. The amount of the discount didn't matter—what swayed the attendees was the very fact that a discount was given. Value attribution kicked in when they received a *discounted* ticket: Regardless of the size of the discount, the patrons regarded the tickets and the productions as inferior.

Knowing how value attribution affects our judgment—and with our anthropologists, the subway riders, hot dog buyers, SoBe drinkers, and theatergoers in tow—we're ready to return to Dean Falk and to the remarkable discovery on the island of Flores. A lot has changed in science since the time of Dubois and Dawson, but as we will see, despite the Piltdown fiasco and the technological advances that followed, modern anthropologists still get swept up by the same force of value attribution.

The groundbreaking news that David Hamlin of National Geographic had to share with Falk was that Mike Morwood had discovered who had crafted the stone tools found on the island of Flores. It turns out that the island effect wasn't just limited to lizards and elephants. Just as there were miniature elephants roaming the island, there were also miniature hominids. It was this previously unknown species that had used the mysterious tools to hunt ancient dwarf elephants.

If the existence of this new species, *Homo floresiensis* (nicknamed "the Hobbit"), could be verified, it would have huge implications: scientists had never before come across any hominid or apelike species that had undergone the island effect. A miniature hominid would constitute a category all by itself. But even more interestingly, the discovery would also add another twist to the unfolding human evolution story: humans and *Homo floresiensis* coexisted as recently as twelve thousand years ago, long after all other hominid species, including Neanderthals, became extinct.

Although Falk was feeling excited, she knew that she had to approach the mystery cautiously and objectively. As she told *National Geographic*, "It's too important not to do right." Falk joined the rest of the team in St. Louis, where the work of investigating the Hobbit began.

At the center of the inquiry was, once again, the brain. Falk hoped to get to the bottom of things by taking what's called an *endocast* of the skull. "An endocast," she explained, "takes up the impressions that the brain left on the walls of the brain case." This cast of the brain captures detailed impressions, which, Falk said, "can be really important and telling."

Though not all skull remains retain enough details to make a good endocast, fortunately, Falk told us, "Hobbit made a gorgeous endocast."

You can almost imagine the scientists holding their breath when the completed endocast came in. The most surprising part of the little brain mock-up was "right at the tip of the front—which would be right where your forehead is, above your nose, an area that is called Brodmann area 10," Falk said. This was an important discovery, because area 10 "is really a very highly advanced part of the brain in living people," Falk explained. "It's where taking initiative happens, planning ahead, silent thought, and daydreaming." The fact that the Hobbit had a complex and well-developed area 10 meant that it was capable of abstract thought.

Falk was amazed: "I've not seen a combination of features like that in any brain, so our interpretation is that it is definitely a small brain, but it's a fancy brain." This was a promising revelation. But the team still hadn't fully verified the existence of a new species. To do so, Falk said, they'd have to compare the Hobbit endocast with every possible alternative: "a human pygmy woman, a chimpanzee female, a normal woman, an adult female *Homo erectus* specimen, and even a human microcephalic—because some people have suggested Hobbits weren't real but pathological *Homo sapiens*."

It came down to a police lineup of sorts. "I could see all of them together and Hobbit in the middle," Falk said. "It looked a whole lot like a *Homo erectus*, which was very exciting. It also shares some features with another group of early hominids. I remember showing that to David Hamlin, and it was this great moment."

Falk and her team took measurements, ran some statistics, and got ready to write up their first paper, which was accepted for publication in *Science*. With the rigorous tests completed and all the alternatives eliminated, Falk was finally convinced. "Based on further studies and also other people's studies of the body," Falk said, "what I think is that the discoverers are correct, that it's a totally new species in the genus *Homo*, that it is a so-called insularly dwarfed species." In other words, it got smaller than its ancestors because it lived on an island. Falk couldn't help but get excited.

"The form of its body is unique; the form of its brain is unique. *Nothing* has been seen like it before."

But rather than embracing the find, modern anthropologists from universities and museums in Australia, Indonesia, and the United States became swayed by value attribution. Taking a page from anthropological history, they doggedly opposed the validity of the Hobbit. They insisted that it was nothing but a microcephalic human. The situation was a replay of what Eugene Dubois had encountered more than a century earlier. "I was a little surprised," Falk recalled, "because I guess I kind of thought, 'Oh well, it's 2004,' and I thought, 'Well, this is a modern day; we've learned a lot since Neanderthal.' So I was surprised at the extent of the acrimony, and the debate—which has gotten quite nasty at times."

Now, it's understandable that anthropologists would have questioned the new findings. Even Falk herself was scientifically cautious before accepting the claim that Hobbit was a new species. But these anthropologists have held out, even in the face of hard data. Meanwhile, the research continues to mount. "We recently did a study on microcephalics," Falk said. "We figured, that's how we'll answer them. We'll image their brain cases, we'll compare Hobbit to them, and we'll *show* that it is not shaped like a microcephalic. And we did that." The study, which used highly advanced statistics, bolstered Falk's previous data.

But despite the new evidence, some scientists still couldn't shake their value attributions. "What they said," Falk recalled, "was, 'Oh, well, your sample size wasn't big enough. We want a bigger sample size of microcephalics.' Well, our sample size was statistically significant and the statistics take sample size into account."

At a certain point, Falk saw that these anthropologists had abandoned science altogether: "Just arguing, 'I don't believe! Maybe there's something out there no one has ever heard of'? It's just not scientific." Falk recalled, "They said, 'Maybe there's some weird form of microcephaly out there that no one discovered yet.'" She was dumbfounded. "How can you argue with that?" Value attribution is such a strong force that it has the power to derail our objective and professional judgment. Simply put, this faction of modern-day anthropologists wasn't thinking scientifically.

If they had been, explained Falk, they would have had to come up with a falsifiable hypothesis. For instance, if the hypothesis is that all tomatoes are red, you can disprove the hypothesis by finding a yellow tomato. "What I said in my paper," Falk told us, "that [the Hobbit] is not a microcephalic, can be falsified with one specimen from a proven microcephalic whose virtual endocast looks identical. And that is scientific."

In the end, it all came down to how the anthropologists ascribed value: an unknown anthropologist, bones from Java, and a too-small brain. Like their predecessors, they couldn't shake the notion that the discovery was too "low-value" to be the real thing.

When the undercurrent of value attribution takes hold, it completely distorts our decision making. And as we'll soon see, it's closely related to another powerful sway—one that can make or break a basketball player's career, win or lose an MIT instructor the favor of his students, and even make us fall in love.

Chapter 4

MICHAEL JORDAN and the FIRST-DATE INTERVIEW

The curse of the low draft pick.

The "cold" professor.

What lovesick college freshmen have in common with HR managers.

When a pretty face equals a higher interest rate.

The "mirror, mirror" effect.

The Joe Friday solution.

t was like picking teams in P.E. Only instead of playground bragging rights, millions of dollars were at stake. And instead of anxious elementary schoolkids, the athletes waiting to be picked were some of the world's best. Welcome to the NBA draft, where choosing the right player can make all the difference.

Pick early and wisely and you can grab a future superstar. That's why NBA teams strike complicated trade deals with each other, vying for the best draft position. It was in just this enviable place that the Portland Trail Blazers found themselves in 1984. They'd finagled the number two position in a year that was especially rich in talent; four of the draftees would later be listed among the top fifty basketball players of all time: eleven-time NBA All-Star Charles Barkley; Hakeem

"The Dream" Olajuwon, who led his team to two back-to-back NBA championships; John Stockton, holder of the all-time NBA record for steals and assists; and a player who needs no introduction, Michael Jordan.

When it was the Blazers' turn to pick, Olajuwon was already spoken for. But the team passed over Michael Jordan and all the other future all-stars, instead selecting Sam Bowie, a talented seven-foot-one player who had shown a lot of promise in college but, because of injuries, would never go on to become an NBA superstar. Since then, Portland has gotten its share of flak for passing on Jordan. They'd visited the biggest candy store in the world and left with a stick of celery.

But before coming down too hard on the Blazers, it's important to realize that the draft is—at its core—educated guesswork and speculation. If we had a time machine, we could go back to the 1980s, load up on Microsoft stock, and give the Blazers' scouts a heads-up about Jordan. Lacking a crystal ball, though, the Blazers did the best they could with the information they had at the time. When it comes down to it, a team can never be exactly sure. Who knew Michael Jordan would become *Michael Jordan*? The draft is just a selection process.

Or is it?

Although none of the participants realized it, the teams were being swayed by the draft long after the selection process had been completed. The evidence is all there, thanks to the league's data collecting practices, which would make the most obsessive accountant proud. From the moment a new player walks onto the court, every aspect of his game—from points scored to number of rebounds, turnovers, fouls, minutes played, and assists—is meticulously recorded. These statistics are a boon to announcers, broadcasters, and fans alike. Buried within this mountain of data, though, are patterns that caught the eye of two economists: Barry Staw and Ha Hoang.

You don't expect economists to sift through sports stats for their data, but there's a lot more going on in the NBA draft than first meets the eye. Staw and Hoang's analysis reveals one of the most alluring sways we've encountered, one that begins at the same source as value attribution, but that diverges from it, pushing us even further from the shore of rationality. Our exploration of this current will help us see how our first impressions of a person can be altered by a mere word, why interviews are a terrible way to determine a job candidate's future performance, and why, sometimes, a pretty face is all it takes to create an offer you can't refuse.

But first let's get inside the heads of basketball team managers. Because so much rides on which player is on the court, it's pretty clear that owners and coaches want to give the most playing time to the most skilled athletes. After all, this isn't elementary school P.E., and you don't have to worry about anyone's mother calling to complain.

Staw and Hoang developed a clever empirical method for judging who the best players are. Dissecting the statistics of 271 new NBA players, they were able to distill all the numbers into three distinct categories that measure skill: *scoring* (points per minute, field-goal percentage, and free-throw percentage); *toughness* (rebounds per minute and blocks per minute); and *quickness* (assists per minute and steals per minute).

If a player is quick, tough, and high-scoring, you'd expect to see him out on the floor a lot. Indeed, when Staw and Hoang ran the data, they confirmed that an athlete's scoring contributed to how much playing time he got. No need to call *Sports Illustrated* with that nugget of data. But the weird thing was that the other two performance factors, toughness and quickness, "had virtually no relationship to the number of minutes a player got to play." Instead, a wholly different, hidden force overshadowed all three of these relevant measurements.

It all came down to that P.E. class moment when players got selected by their respective teams. Staw and Hoang found that the variable most responsible for an NBA player's time on the court—"above and beyond any effects of a player's performance, injury, or trade status"—was his *draft selection order*. Even after controlling for all other factors, in a given season "every increment in the draft number [e.g., getting drafted ninth instead of eighth] decreased playing time by as much as 23 minutes." Incredibly, draft order continued to predict playing time all the way through a player's fifth year in the NBA, the final year measured in the study.

But draft order had even deeper implications. Being picked late in the draft increased a player's likelihood of getting traded to another team and ultimately affected the longevity of his career. "A first-round draft pick," found Staw and Hoang, "stayed in the league approximately 3.3 years longer than a player drafted in the second round."

Now remember, Staw and Hoang had isolated draft order from all the other variables. That means that if you have two players with the exact same toughness, scoring, and quickness record, the one picked earlier in the draft would get more playing time, be much less likely to be traded, and have a longer career than his counterpart, who—although he turned out to be just as good—had the misfortune of being picked later in the draft.

Let's pause here. Are Staw and Hoang saying what we think they're saying? If we think about this rationally, once a player is picked, his draft order shouldn't matter. After all, coaches and managers should only be interested in a player's level of productivity on the court and his overall fit within the team. Once the draft is over, the draft number becomes an arbitrary statistic that gives no indication of how he'll actually perform on his new team.

But here's where value attribution meets up with a sway called the diagnosis bias—our propensity to label people, ideas, or things based on our initial opinions of them—and our inability to reconsider those judgments once we've made them. In other words, once a player is tagged as a "low pick," most coaches let that diagnosis cloud their entire perception of him. It's as if each athlete wears a permanent price tag on his jersey. Score points, catch a lot of rebounds, block shots, and make steals, and it still won't affect your playing time as much as your draft order does, even years down the road.

None of us is immune to falling into the same trap that snared the NBA coaches. Imagine, for example, that you needed to hire an attorney and had a choice between one who'd finished at the top of her class and her classmate who'd finished sixth. The top-ranked one would be much more appealing—even if the sixth-ranked one was equally competent and might end up being a better fit for your particular needs. Even after you made the hire, it would be impossible to let go of your awareness of class rank and keep it from affecting your perception of the lawyer's competence. Every time something seemed to be going wrong, in the back of your mind you'd think, "I bet the top-ranked one would have done things differently."

We are so susceptible to this diagnostic sway, in fact, that even a single, seemingly innocuous, word has the power to change our opinions. To see this in action, let's head to MIT, where the students of Economics 70 thought they had reason to relax. They had just been seated when a college representative walked in and told them that their professor was out of town that day. But before they had time to pack up their books, they were told that a substitute instructor would be filling in, an instructor they had never met. The representative from the college explained to them that "since we of Economics 70 are interested in the general problem of how various classes react to different instructors, we're going to have an instructor today you've never had before." At the end of the period, they would be asked to fill out some forms about the sub. But first, to give them a sense of who this mysterious guy was, the students received a brief bio describing him.

What they didn't know was that there were actually two different bios being handed out. Half the students received this version:

Mr. —— is a graduate student in the Department of Economics and Social Science here at MIT. He has had three semesters of teaching experience in psychology at another college. This is his first semester teaching Ec 70. He is 26 years old, a veteran, and married. People who know him consider him to be a very warm person, industrious, critical, practical, and determined.

The second half received a nearly identical bio. Only two words had been changed:

Mr. —— is a graduate student in the Department of Economics and Social Science here at MIT. He has had three semesters of teaching experience in psychology at another college. This is his first semester teaching Ec 70. He is 26 years old, a veteran, and married. People who know him consider him to be a rather cold person, industrious, critical, practical, and determined.

The difference, of course, is that half the bios describe the professor as "very warm" while the second half describe him as "rather cold." Remember that the students were under the impression that they had all read the same description. Now enter the substitute, who spent the rest of the period leading a discussion about material the class had recently covered.

At the end of the period, each student received an identical questionnaire about the sub. Upon seeing the results, you'd think the students were responding to two completely different instructors. Most students in the group that had received the bio describing the substitute as "warm" loved him. They described the instructor as "good natured, considerate of others, informal, sociable, popular, humorous, and humane." Although the second group sat in the exact same class and participated in the exact same discussion, a majority of them didn't really take to the instructor. They saw him as "self-centered, formal, unsociable, unpopular, irritable, humorless, and ruthless."

This one word, "warm" or "cold"—albeit irrelevant in the larger scheme of things—made students assign a high or low value to the professor. Like the NBA teams with the draft order, once the students read the substitute's bio, their opinions of him were set.

In other words, a single word has the power to alter our whole perception of another person—and possibly sour the relationship before it even begins. When we hear a description of someone, no matter how brief, it inevitably shapes our experience of that person.

Think how often we diagnose a person based on a casual

description. Imagine you're set up on a blind date with a friend of a friend. When the big night arrives, you meet your date at a restaurant and make small talk while you wait for the appetizer to arrive. "So," you say, "what do you have planned for this weekend?" "Oh, probably what I do every weekend: stay home and read Hegel," your date responds with a straight face. Because your mutual friend described your date as "smart, funny, and interesting," you laugh, thinking to yourself that your friend was right, this person's deadpan sense of humor is right up your alley. And just like that, the date is off to a promising start. But what if the friend had described your date as "smart, *serious*, and interesting"? In that light, you might interpret the comment as genuine and instead think, "How much Hegel can one person read?" Your entire perception of your date would be clouded; you'd spend the rest of dinner wracking your brain over the difference between Heidegger and Hegel and leave without ordering dessert.

Interestingly, even when we're not given a clear-cut value tag, we are so eager to assign a value that we create our own diagnostic labels. Most of us simply can't stay neutral for long, which is why we're so susceptible to following the siren song of the diagnostic bias.

Each day we're bombarded with so much information that if we had no way to filter it, we'd be unable to function. Psychologist Franz Epting, an expert in understanding how people construct meaning in their experiences, explained, "We use diagnostic labels to organize and simplify. But any

classification that you come up with," cautioned Epting, "has got to work by ignoring a lot of other things—with the hope that the things you are ignoring don't make a difference. And that's where the rub is. Once you get a label in mind, you don't notice things that don't fit within the categories that do make a difference."

What Epting is saying is that all of us put on diagnostic glasses when we encounter new people. When we meet someone at a party, for example, we quickly diagnose him or her as "approachable" or "standoffish" before deciding whether we want to engage in a conversation.

But we pay a price for these mental shortcuts, explained Epting: "The baggage that comes with labeling is the notion of the blinders, really. It prevents you from seeing what's clearly before your face; all you're seeing now is the label." An NBA player is labeled as a low draft pick. Thanks to our diagnostic bias, it doesn't matter whether he plays his heart out: he'll always be viewed as subpar. Once a professor is described as cold, his personality and teaching ability cease to matter: his students dislike him anyway. The diagnosis bias causes us to distort or even ignore objective data.

No one knows about the power of these diagnostic distortions better than Professor Allen Huffcutt, who for the better part of twenty years has studied one of the most important diagnostic moments we encounter: the job interview.

When you think about it, the standard job interview is a lot like a first date. As Huffcutt explained, "You don't have a clear format to follow and you just let the interview go as it will." Sitting across from a candidate, managers try to form an impression: Does the candidate share my interests? How's the chemistry between us? Is there a connection? "If you look across all industries," Huffcutt told us, "this unstructured interview format is by far the most dominant form of applicant selection."

It's easy to understand why companies would be so drawn to the "first-date" interview format. After all, a manager will be spending a lot of time with the person they hire; they want to make sure the person is a good fit. And, Huffcutt explained, "We have a notion of the ideal employee that we want to hire."

Ideally, of course, companies would have a magic box that could perfectly predict a potential candidate's performance. Drop in a few facts about a hire, add a sampling of their skills and—voilà—out comes a score indicating how good an employee the candidate would be. As it turns out, this notion isn't as fanciful as we might think.

There's a whole segment of academics fascinated with hiring practices. Every year, Huffcutt makes a pilgrimage to a conference where he and his colleagues review all the latest studies about hiring practices. Over the years, Huffcutt and his colleagues have examined a host of specific selection criteria and determined their relevance to actual job performance—and through this process, they have, in essence, created the elusive "magic box" of job candidate competence.

The contents of this box, assembled through meticulous research, would be a gold mine for anyone making a hiring decision. But when we look inside, what we see comes as a complete surprise. Explained Huffcutt, "Your typical unstructured interview"—the common "first-date" method—"just doesn't do well. We have a long history of research confirming that."

Just how "not well" is surprising. When researchers conducted a meta-analysis—a broad study incorporating data from every scientific work ever conducted in the field—they found that there's only a small correlation between first-date (unstructured) job interviews and job performance. The marks managers give job candidates have very little to do with how well those candidates actually perform on the job.

It all comes back to the dating analogy. "How many people go on a first date," Huffcutt reflected, "get a certain impression, keep dating the person, and then, over time, see the reality of the person? That first impression can be totally wrong. You later wonder, 'What in the world was I thinking? How did I not see these things?' Well, the same thing happens in the interview. You've got a very limited time exposure, applicants put on their best show, managers put on their best show, and—not surprisingly—you just don't see the realities of the person in twenty minutes."

In this way, professional hiring managers have a lot in common with college students sitting in their dorm rooms, daydreaming about their girlfriend or boyfriend. As two Canadian psychologists, Tara MacDonald and Mike Ross, recently discovered, students dismiss objective data when the information doesn't fit what they want to see. In their study,

MacDonald and Ross talked to college students during one of the most exciting times in their lives: as college freshmen who'd recently become involved in a new romantic relationship.

The researchers asked the students to assess the quality of their relationships—everything from trust to commitment to communication to overall level of satisfaction. Then they asked each student: Do you think you'll be together with your partner in two months? How about in six months? In a year? In five years? Do you see yourselves getting married? Do you think you are going to be together for the rest of your life?

Now, we've all been there: in a new relationship, head over heels in love, feeling on top of the world. Of course the students tended to be optimistic about their relationship's prospects. But then, continuing with the inquiry, the researchers asked permission to reach out to each student's roommate and family and ask them what *they* thought about the quality of the relationship and how long it would last. These people were observing the relationships from the outside, without new love's rose-colored glasses. Indeed, across the board, students were more optimistic about the relationship's prospects than were their roommates. Least optimistic of all were the parents.

A semester of college life passed by—classes and parties were attended, fights were had. When MacDonald and Ross revisited the students six months later, 61 percent of them were still in the relationship. Six months after that—a year after the original interviews—the number of students still involved with the same partner had further decreased to 48 percent.

When they analyzed the results, MacDonald and Ross found that judgmental roommates and nosy parents really do know best—well, sort of. Roommates and parents were far better than students at predicting a relationship's longevity. But, surprisingly, what MacDonald and Ross discovered was that even when the students predicted their relationships would be long-lived, their assessments of the *problems* in their relationships were right on the money. The students weren't blind to the issues that were already putting strains on the relationships; they simply ignored them when it came to making predictions about the future. Overwhelmingly, whether students detected the early warning signs or not, they overestimated the relationship's longevity. This dismissal of the facts is the first of three types of mistakes, or traps, we all fall into when we diagnose.

It's a trap you might be familiar with if you've ever been in the market for a new home. You see an ad for a house in a neighborhood you love, maybe on a tree-lined street you make it a point to drive along on your commute. You make an appointment with a real-estate agent right away, convinced that *this* is your dream home.

When you actually see it, the house turns out to be a little less dreamy than you'd originally imagined—the bathrooms need to be gutted, you've seen closets bigger than two of the bedrooms, and the backyard looks like a jungle. But given that you've already judged it a dream house, are you more apt to focus on the house's faults or sigh over its spacious front porch, shiny hardwood floors, and Jacuzzi tubs?

It's understandable that lovesick college students would twist information to convince themselves that their relationship is going to last or that prospective homeowners involved in the emotionally charged process of buying a new home might behave less rationally than usual. But you'd expect professional managers selecting new employees to be more level-headed. As it turns out, however, Huffcutt explained, managers are especially prone to ignoring highly relevant information when it comes to hiring. While the infatuated students are blinded by optimism, hiring managers, according to Huffcutt, "just ask poor questions."

The standard job interview questions are familiar to all of us. But they make Huffcutt cringe. During our conversation with him, he shared a list of the top ten most commonly asked questions during an interview. You'd think that, given the frequency with which they're asked, at least *some* of them would be useful. But of the whole list, Huffcutt gave a passing mark to only one question. See if you can guess which one it is.

1. Why should I hire you?
2. What do you see yourself doing five years from now?
3. What do you consider to be your greatest strengths and weaknesses?
4. How would you describe yourself?

5. What college subject did you like the best and the least?
6. What do you know about our company?
7. Why did you decide to seek a job with our company?
8. Why did you leave your last job?
9. What do you want to earn five years from now?
10. What do you really want to do in life?

When we look at these questions more closely, we see that they cluster around specific themes. The first group is taken from the Barbara Walters school of interviewing. The idea behind questions 1, 3, and 4 is that by asking semi-insightful, self-evaluative questions, you can get a sense of the *real* candidate. This approach might make for a good episode of *20/20*, but it doesn't glean useful information about what the candidate would *really* be like on the job.

Take question 3, about the candidate's greatest strengths and weaknesses. "What do you really gain by asking that?" Huffcutt pointed out, "Who's going to tell you their true weaknesses? I'm not going to say, 'Well, you know, sometimes I stay out too late at night drinking and I'm late for work.' Who's going to say that?" As Huffcutt pointed out, "Applicants would likely have prepared for these types of questions and thought about them and developed a standard, pat answer. They're going to say something that sounds good but doesn't really portray a weakness: 'Sometimes I try to do things too well' or 'Sometimes I take my work too seriously.' "

Likewise, question 1 ("Why should I hire you?") is the equivalent of Walters asking a presidential candidate, "Why should we elect you?" If the question sounds rehearsed, so will the answer. "Obviously, any applicant worth their salt would come up with a nice answer for that," said Huffcutt with a shrug. Question 4 ("How would you describe yourself?") is "another one that's not going to do much." Stating that you're an enthusiastic, hardworking team player doesn't carry much predictive value about your ability to carry out and complete tasks. At its core, the problem with the Barbara Walters constellation is that the questions elicit prepackaged responses that don't really tell us anything about the candidate's actual skills.

The second group, composed of questions 2, 9, and 10, requires candidates to gaze into the future. But unless they're applying for a job at a psychic hotline, their predictions carry little weight. Even more problematic is that applicants can be—shall we say—less than forthcoming about their true plans—a little like the blind date who assures you that their current dead-end job is "just a stepping stone." Look at question 2, about what you see yourself doing in five years. As Huffcutt pointed out, "Everybody is going to come up with a nice-sounding answer: 'I want to be advancing in the company; I want to be working toward higher levels.' Everyone is going to say something that sounds deep."

The final cluster, questions 5, 7, and 8, takes the opposite approach and turns the interviewer into a historian. The thing is, though, when people revisit the past they often reconstruct it. Questions like number 7 ("Why did you decide to seek a job with our company?") invite artful responses.

"Once again, who's going to give a truthful answer? 'I'm desperate, the bills are piling up, I need a job, and you have an
opening,'" Huffcutt asked. Instead, "they're going to come
up with some nice-sounding answer."

And the winner (by default) is unassuming question 6
("What do you know about our company?"). "That can actually be a decent question," explained Huffcutt. "That gets
into whether they took the time to research your company,
which can be a good sign—at least better than the previous
questions." Number 6 is still not the best of questions, but it
does provide *some* helpful information.

All of the other top ten questions invite a performance by
the candidate: "I work too hard . . . I'm a team player who
enjoys a good challenge . . . My life's dream is to work for
your company . . . in this exact job." Yeah, that's the ticket.

Although everyone from the lowliest worker to the CEO
knows that these performance charades are going on, hiring
managers are attracted to the first-date format, thinking that
a good conversation will allow their instincts to guide them
to the right candidate. "There is a strong feeling," Huffcutt
explained, "that you can't achieve accuracy in selection without going through the interview." We want to really sniff
out that perfect candidate and get the sensation that, yes, this
is the right person for the job.

The reason managers can err so easily is that, in addition
to ignoring objective data, they focus on and give too much
credence to irrelevant factors, which is the second trap we all
fall into when making a judgment. It's a trap familiar to any-

one who's ever bought a bottle of wine solely because of the attractiveness of the label or picked an accountant based on the appearance of his office.

Interestingly, the purveyors of act-now, special-offer junk mail can shed light on this behavior. Take what happened in South Africa when a consumer lending bank wanted to push personal loans to fifty thousand of its customers. Working together with a team of economists, the bank crafted several variations on the same basic loan offer letter. The different versions were randomly assigned to recipients and mailed off without any indication that the letters were part of an experiment.

The letters included different interest rates (ranging from 3.25% to 7.75% per *month*); some featured a comparison to a competitor's rate; others a giveaway ([Win one of] TEN CELL PHONES UP FOR GRABS EACH MONTH!); and still others a photo of either a man's or a woman's pleasant, smiling face.

Now, you'd think that the customer would evaluate the offer based purely on interest rate and the specific terms of the loan. Marketing gimmicks such as competitor comparisons, giveaway offers, and fanciful photos shouldn't be part of the calculation. Indeed, the comparison to a competitor's offer didn't really affect the would-be customers. Similarly, throwing in an opportunity to win a cell phone didn't have much of an overall effect. The unexpected effect kicked in with the least relevant variation: the inclusion of a picture of the smiling face in the corner. Men who received a picture of one of four smiling *women* were much more likely to sign up for the loan than were the men who received a picture of a smiling *man*. According to the study, the magnitude of this effect is "about as much as dropping the interest rate 4.5 percentage points." Obviously, having a picture of a pretty woman on a letter doesn't make for a better financial offer, but researchers speculated that the men were attracted to the woman and therefore signed up for the loan.

Let's take a step back here. It's unlikely that any man would consciously sign up for a higher-interest loan just because the offer letter had a picture of a woman on it. But just like the college freshmen who misdiagnosed the longevity of their relationships because they ignored valuable information about the quality of their relationships, the loan customers made diagnostic errors in evaluating the attractiveness of the loan because they didn't focus on the important data.

Imagine how many buying decisions we make for similarly irrelevant reasons—do we really think that we'll get a better deal or product from a company whose ad features a spokes-gecko or a "priceless" slogan?

Swayed by the picture of the woman, the South African bank customers were prone to diagnose the loan offer as attractive, in the same way that the MIT students were swayed by the description of the substitute professor as "warm" and NBA teams were swayed by a player's draft order.

Huffcutt's work on job interviews shed an interesting light on one of the more intriguing aspects of the diagnosis bias, one that we might consider dubbing the "mirror, mirror" effect. When we conduct job interviews, said Huffcutt, "we often base the image of the ideal candidate on ourselves. Somebody comes in who's similar to us, and we're going to click; we're probably going to want to hire them." But, of course, there's no proof that just because potential employees are similar to their manager, they'll be a better fit for the company. In fact, there's a compelling case to be made that managers would be better off hiring someone *unlike* them— so that where the manager falls short, the new hire can pick up the slack.

Still, managers have a difficult time turning their backs on the "first-date" job interview. "Everybody thinks they have this ability to see an applicant and make a great decision, truly understand them," explained Huffcutt. "Everybody thinks they can do that, and that's part of the problem. It's hard to convince somebody that they're not doing as well as they think."

This tendency is by no means limited to managers who do the hiring. We all diagnose when encountering a person or situation for the first time, and study after study shows we're not very good at it. And yet, whether we're interviewing a potential candidate or entering a new relationship, time and again we overestimate our ability to form an objective opinion.

If we can't overcome the diagnosis bias outright, we can take a cue from mythology and adopt Odysseus's strategy. Knowing that he wouldn't be able to help but follow the sirens' song, jump from the ship, and drown, he had his crew tie him to the mast.

When it comes to interviews, managers need to restrain themselves from delving into first-date questions and focus instead on specific past experience and "job-related hypothetical scenarios," said Huffcutt. It's the Joe Friday, just-the-facts-ma'am approach. The idea is to focus on relevant data and squelch any questions that invite the candidate to predict the future, reconstruct the past, or ponder life's big questions. It's all about the important information. What kind of accounting software are you familiar with? What experience do you have running PR campaigns? How would you reduce inefficiencies on the assembly line?

Because they confine managers to specifics, these structured interviews fare much better than their unstructured counterparts. The meta-analysis showed that "Joe Friday" interviews are *six times* more effective than first-date interviews at predicting a candidate's job performance.

But even then interviews aren't that great as a predictive tool, because some people simply know how to sell themselves better than others. As counterintuitive as it sounds, you don't need interviews at all. Research shows that an aptitude test predicts performance just as well as a structured interview.

"But then again," Huffcutt pointed out, "everybody expects an interview." Huffcutt's solution is to turn the process on its head. "Given that the applicant is expecting an interview," he offered, "the ideal system is to use the higher accuracy techniques up front to make your decision—things like mental ability tests, work samples." Then, "when you've identified your top candidates," he advised, "you use an unstructured interview to really sell them on taking the job, get them excited about the company. You can use it for some very useful things, just not for the hiring decision itself."

The point is, when we're in the position to make a diagnosis, we *all* become overly confident in our predictive abilities and overly optimistic about the future. Like the students in rocky relationships who believed love would prevail, we often ignore all evidence that contradicts what we want to believe.

While the Odysseus approach might help us avoid asking the kinds of questions that lead us to incorrectly diagnose a person or situation, Huffcutt makes it clear that it's harder to overcome this sway than we might think.

When we asked him whether his own department had made any changes in its hiring procedures based on his research, Huffcutt smiled. "That's a great question," he said, "and the answer is no. I've made some suggestions on how we can do better on interviews, but so far they haven't been taken."

Chapter ⁵

The BIPOLAR EPIDEMIC and the CHAMELEON EFFECT

A psychiatric outbreak.

↓↓↓↓↓
Sugar pills and Prozac.

↓↓↓↓
Tricking Israeli army commanders.

↓↓↓
How to sound beautiful.

↓↓
How old do you feel?

↓
The love bridge.

t had the makings of an epidemic. From 1994 to 2003 the number of children diagnosed with bipolar disorder—a condition characterized by cycles of devastating hopelessness and despair followed by times of ecstatic excitement—had skyrocketed. In 1994 only twenty-five of every hundred thousand American kids under the age of nineteen were diagnosed as bipolar. But by 2003 the number of cases had shot up by a staggering *forty times*. A doubling of this rare but serious condition would have been newsworthy in its own right, but a fortyfold increase made it clear *something* was going on. The question was what.

One explanation is that there was a surge in the number of kids suffering from the disorder. But the diagnosis of 800,000 children in 2003 alone, compared with 20,000 per year just a decade earlier, signaled a radical change—a fundamental shift, perhaps, in the process of growing up. But no such change had been identified. Moreover, because bipolar disorder involves a heightened risk of suicide, if its occurrence had increased, we'd expect to see a corresponding spike in suicide and attempted suicide rates among young people. Over this same period, though, suicide rates among America's children didn't rise at all—in fact, they went *down* by 23 percent.

Another explanation is that the number of kids with bipolar disorder had always been large, but that in the last decade more parents had begun to seek psychiatric help for their children. The problem with this theory is that if there had been a massive stampede to psychiatrists, it stands to reason that diagnoses of disorders other than bipolar would have increased as well. But there was no such surge.

And this brings us to the third possible explanation: if the number of children suffering from bipolar disorder hadn't increased, and the number of parents seeking psychiatric help for their kids hadn't increased, maybe all that had changed was the number of children being *diagnosed*. Not only does our exploration of this theory take us deeper into the two diagnosis traps we explored in the last chapter, it also uncovers a new and powerful trap that affects both the person with the bias and the person being diagnosed.

It turns out that even the medical community is not immune to the lure of the diagnosis bias. As the job interviewers taught us, one of the traps in diagnosing is that we tend to rely on arbitrary information. To understand how this force contributed to the bipolar epidemic, we must cross an ocean and travel back in time to the tumultuous world of pre–World War II Germany. There a psychiatrist named Emil Kraepelin was developing the first categorization scheme for mental disorders. Instead of relying on objective, scientific data, Kraepelin used his own intuitive judgment to arrive at the diagnostic scheme. Some of the labels he developed are still used today, including manic-depressive disorder, also known as bipolar disorder. Some of his other diagnoses, however, are more obscure and, frankly, unnerving—such as his category of "individuals with distinctly hysterical traits," which included "dreamers and poets, swindlers and Jews."

Nonetheless, psychiatrists found Kraepelin's diagnostic system to be a useful tool (he's regarded as the father of modern psychiatry) because it created an analog to the medical model of diagnosing diseases. If a patient visits a physician and complains of a sore throat, headache, and fever, the doctor can do a quick examination, diagnose strep throat, and administer the prescribed remedy. Similarly, under Kraepelin's system, a patient who sees a psychiatrist and exhibits symptoms of bipolar disorder can be diagnosed and assigned a course of treatment, be it therapy or medication. This medical model of diagnosis has proven popular with psychiatrists up through the present day.

In 1980 the new edition of the *Diagnostic and Statistical Manual of Mental Disorders* (DSM-III) broadened the definition of bipolar disorder to include individuals with less pronounced symptoms. No longer did the diagnosis require previous hospitalization for a manic episode. The new diagnostic now included such commonplace descriptors as "feel[ing] sad or empty"; "appear[ing] tearful"; exhibiting "fatigue," "indecision," or "insomnia"; being "more talkative than usual"; suffering from "distractibility"; or having "inflated self-esteem." Even individuals who met only some of these criteria could now be included under the bipolar umbrella.

On top of that, as British psychiatrist David Healy explained, in the 1990s pharmaceutical companies increasingly began to draw attention to this formerly rare and relatively unknown condition. Their campaign included the publication of new journals, the establishment of bipolar societies and annual conferences, television commercials for new treatments, and frequent workshops for mental health providers. During that time it was difficult for either parents or therapists to avoid hearing talk of bipolar disorder. What followed, said Dr. Healy, was a snowball effect. The more bipolar disorder was placed in the spotlight, the more clinicians were exposed to it, the higher the diagnosis rate climbed, which in turn led to further diagnosing. Factor in the new symptom standards for the illness, and the bipolar epidemic became so widespread that a Massachusetts hospital treated groups of preschoolers. Healy reported that even a two-year-old has been diagnosed with the disorder.

Now, the bipolar designation was arbitrary for a few reasons: Kraepelin had relied on his own perceptions, rather than on hard science, when categorizing the mental disorders; the

DSM-III broadened his original definition in 1980; and pharmaceutical marketing campaigns since then had attempted to bring more people into the fold. Primed to be on the lookout for bipolar disorder, psychiatrists started seeing it everywhere they looked. What many of them failed to recognize was that they had fallen into one of the traps of the diagnosis bias—arbitrarily assigning labels.

On its own, relying on arbitrary information causes enough problems, but this inclination is further complicated by the other trap of diagnosis: our tendency to ignore objective data that contradicts our initial diagnosis. To gain a deeper understanding of how this trap plays out, we talked with psychologist Bruce Wampold. Dr. Wampold is the kind of man who believes in empirical, quantitative evidence and objective data. He used his degree in mathematics and his psychological training to analyze what it is that makes psychotherapy work. His adherence to quantitative evidence meant that Wampold had to rely on large enough sets of data to make sure he was capturing all the relevant factors. It was only after taking into account every relevant scientific study on the effectiveness of psychotherapy that he began his meta-analysis.

The typical study that Wampold reviewed and analyzed looked something like this: A group of real-life patients who had sought therapy for a variety of reasons were randomly placed with different therapists, some of whom subscribed to a "medical diagnosis" theoretical model, and others of whom didn't. After the period of therapy ended, the clients were questioned about their lives and emotional states. They were asked whether their concerns had been alleviated and what their overall experience of therapy had been. Replications and variations of this experiment conducted with thousands of clients and hundreds of therapists produced a rich data set for Wampold. When he crunched the numbers, the results were surprising.

Wampold's findings showed that there were three distinct elements that made a psychotherapist successful. The first and most straightforward was talent. Just as there are good and bad managers, some therapists are more skilled than others. Some of the clinicians—regardless of theoretical orientation—stood out as highly effective and successful in treating their clients. The second element Wampold identified is what's called "therapeutic alliance"—the quality of the relationship the practitioner formed with the client. Therapists who had good relationships with their clients tended to have more positive results than those who didn't. The third factor was whether the studies allowed the therapists to use the method of therapy with which they felt most comfortable.

Surprisingly, diagnosis didn't figure into the equation one way or the other. That is, clients who were treated by a therapist who used the medical model were no better or worse off than their counterparts who saw practitioners who *didn't* use the medical model. As Wampold told us when we interviewed him, "diagnosis is irrelevant; it doesn't matter what the diagnosis is. You can go through the diagnoses—depression, panic, PTSD—and it doesn't matter. The whole notion of certain treatments for specific disorders falls apart." That is, "it's not the particular treatment that's making the difference; it's the ability of the therapist to work with the patient, creating a collaborative bond."

To be clear, Wampold is not claiming that psychotherapy isn't effective. His meta-analysis actually found that it had very positive mental health effects. Neither does he believe that therapists who subscribe to the medical model don't do a good job. His comprehensive research simply points out that the diagnostic model doesn't have any therapeutic advantage in and of itself.

Now, returning to the apparent epidemic of bipolar disorder, one could argue that despite aggressive diagnosing, children were benefiting from being prescribed medications for bipolar disorder. Indeed, officials from the Centers for Disease Control have argued that the introduction of selective serotonin reuptake inhibitors (SSRIs) such as Prozac, Paxil, Celexa, and Zoloft during the 1990s was the reason for the reduction in suicide rates. As the argument goes, children treated with SSRIs were less likely to feel depressed and commit suicide.

But a closer look at the data reveals a different picture. In 2002 a group of researchers analyzed all FDA medical and statistical data about the efficacy of SSRIs. They looked at "47 randomized placebo controlled short-term efficacy trials" conducted on the major SSRI drugs. Their conclusion stunned the psychiatric community. It turned out that when all the studies were aggregated and all the data meticulously analyzed, SSRIs were no more clinically effective than placebos in making patients—either kids or adults—feel better. That is, sugar pills and Prozac had about the same therapeutic effect.

Dr. David Antonuccio, professor of psychiatry and behavioral sciences at the University of Nevada, explained to us, "When it comes to SSRIs and children, only three out of the sixteen randomized control trials they had for kids showed a positive result. *Only three out of sixteen.* And of course there is also the risk of serious side effects."

Although the hard data had shown that the medical model of diagnosing served no therapeutic purpose (Wampold's study was published in 1997) and that the SSRI drugs are clinically ineffective, psychiatrists nevertheless kept diagnosing and prescribing. Once even the most seasoned professionals begin diagnosing, it's very hard to stop.

But there's another aspect to diagnosis we have yet to explore—its effects on the person being diagnosed. What about those kids who have been diagnosed as bipolar? What are the potential effects of such a diagnosis? To investigate this dynamic and uncover the third and most surprising trap of diagnosis, let's head to Israel, where 105 soldiers were about to participate in a grueling fifteen-week commander training program. It was a rigorous and intense process, requiring harsh physical training, mental concentration, and sixteen-hour workdays.

The would-be commanders didn't know it, but this partic-

SWAY

ular course was going to be different from any to date. Before this session's classes started, psychologist Dov Eden informed the training officers leading the program that the army had accumulated comprehensive data on each of the trainees, including, Eden explained, "psychological test scores, socio-metric data from the previous course, and ratings by previous commanders."

Based on this comprehensive information, Eden told the officers, each soldier had been classified into one of three "command potential" (CP) categories: "high," "regular," and "unknown" (due to insufficient information). Trainees from each classification were divided equally into the four trainee classes. "You will copy each trainee's CP," Eden told the offi-cers, "into his personal record. You are requested to learn your trainees' names and their predicted CP by the beginning of the course."

The trainees, of course, had no idea that any of this was going on. And the officers didn't know that the so-called command potential, along with all the supporting data, was completely bogus. Scores were randomly assigned to the trainees and had nothing to do with their intelligence, past performance, or ability.

Nonetheless, when Eden returned fifteen weeks later, he discovered something remarkable. At the end of the course, the soldiers took a paper-and-pencil test that measured their new knowledge of "combat tactics, topography, standard op-erating procedures, and such practical skills as navigation and accuracy of weapon firing." This test wasn't rigged; it was part of normal procedure, a standardized assessment all soldiers took at the end of their training. But this is where the effects of assigning soldiers to the different command potential categories became apparent. The soldiers whom the training officers *thought* had a high CP score performed much better on the test (scoring an average of 79.98) than their "unknown" and "regular" counterparts (who scored 72.43 and 65.18, respectively). Simply being labeled, however arbitrarily, as having high leadership potential translated directly into actual improved ability—improved by a staggering 22.7 percent. Remember, neither the trainers nor the trainees had any idea what was going on. Without realizing it, the trainees had taken on the characteristics of the diagnoses ascribed to them.

This kind of phenomenon is by no means limited to the military. A meta-analysis conducted by psychologists at SUNY Albany suggested that these same diagnostic effects operate in the workplace. If you've ever been fortunate enough to work for a boss who values and believes in you, you'll know that you tend to rise to meet the high expectations set for you. On the other hand, there's nothing that will make you feel more incompetent and demoralized than a supervisor who is convinced you don't have what it takes.

The same phenomenon can occur when a psychologist or psychiatrist assigns a label to a client, be it bipolar disorder, anxiety, or depression. As Wampold explained, one of the problems inherent in diagnoses is that "there's pressure to make everything fit with that diagnosis, so once that diagnosis has been made, all the behaviors and decisions become confir-matory." When a child who has been branded as bipolar appears "tearful" or feels "sad or empty," these emotions get interpreted as part of the condition. When we are labeled, explained psychologist Franz Epting, "it's easy to start acting it out as a way of being in the world." We fit into the mold created by the diagnosis. "And then it becomes quite a tangle between what's *really* going on with us versus what we have been labeled with."

In other words, this molding process becomes self-perpetuating: when we take on characteristics assigned to us, the diagnosis is reinforced and reaffirmed. Take a look at what happened with the Israeli soldiers and officers. When Eden informed the trainers that the command potential scores had actually been fabricated and assigned randomly, they staunchly disagreed. In a desperate attempt to prove their point, they offered up evidence that the high-potential soldiers indeed performed better on the exit exams. This, of course, is circular logic. The exit tests confirmed the initial diagnosis; the trainees had merely molded their abilities to the diagnoses ascribed to them.

And this is the third trap of diagnosis: when we brand or label people, they take on the characteristics of the diagnosis. In psychological circles, this mirroring of expectations is known as the Pygmalion effect (describing how we take on positive traits assigned to us by someone else) and the Golem effect (describing how we take on negative traits). But let's use "chameleon effect" as our catchall term. This phenomenon helps to explain why fifty-one women waiting for the phone to ring had a lot in common with the soldiers in the Israeli commander training study. The women had signed up for a study on communication; all they knew about it was that they would be having a short conversation with a randomly selected man. When the phone finally rang, the women engaged in seemingly ordinary chitchat—they talked about the weather and their college majors, the kinds of things you'd expect a couple of strangers to discuss. But unbeknownst to the women, they were engaged in a hidden dance.

The prelude to the dance had begun a few minutes earlier. The men on the other end of the line had also signed up for a communication study. But unlike the women, each man, before calling the woman, had received a "biographical information form" and a snapshot of her. What the men didn't know was that although the bios were accurate, the pictures were not. In fact, they were photos of completely different women, specially selected by the researchers beforehand. Half of these fake photos were of very pretty women, while the other half were of women who were more ordinary in appearance. Each bio was randomly assigned one of the photos.

You don't have to be a psychologist to guess that while the men gave the bios a quick read, they took a good, hard look at the photos. After reviewing the bio and the photo—but before actually talking to his assigned partner—each man was handed an "Impression Formation Questionnaire," which asked him to rate his expectations about her.

The results of the survey were telling. Regardless of what

the bios said, men who saw pictures of pretty women expected to interact with "sociable, poised, humorous, and socially adept women." The other group of men—the ones who thought they'd be talking to less attractive partners— thought the women would be "unsociable, awkward, serious, and socially inept."

Once each man had formed an opinion, it was hard for him to see the woman in any other light. And, as you can imagine, the men brought these biases into their phone conversations.

Meanwhile, the women were still sitting alone in their rooms. They had no idea that the men had been shown pictures—real or otherwise. When they were connected with the men, they simply engaged in casual chitchat.

And this is where the experiment *really* began. The researchers recorded the calls, then edited out the men's side of the conversations. The resulting clips, containing only the women's voices, were played to a third, independent group of twelve ordinary people, who knew nothing at all about the study and had never met any of the other participants. This fresh group was completely unaware of any biases the men may have held.

Listening to *just* the women's side of the conversations, this jury was asked to evaluate each woman using the same Impression Formation Questionnaire the men had filled out earlier.

Remarkably, without knowing it, the jury members cut in on the mysterious dance that had taken place between the men and the women. They attributed the same traits to the women based on their *voices alone* that the men had attributed to them based on their (fake) *photos*.

How did the jury come to the same conclusion? After all, they never met any of the participants, saw any of the snapshots, or were told about the men's biases. They didn't get to listen to the men speak and were completely in the dark about the nature of the study.

The answer lies with the subtle power of the chameleon effect. Remember that before the men had exchanged a single word with the "beautiful" women, they already thought of them as socially graceful, funny, composed, and collected.

Once the men formed this opinion, it affected every aspect of how they interacted with the women. Imagine if you were talking on the phone to someone whom you believed to be attractive. You'd likely be more engaged, listen more actively, and generally find yourself more immersed in the interaction.

When the "beautiful" women spoke with their mysterious strangers, they couldn't help but react to the cues the men were sending. Without realizing it, they took on the characteristics that the men had expected them to have. The researchers explained, "What had initially been reality in the minds of the men had now become reality in the behavior of the women." The women unconsciously picked up on the "beautiful" opinion the men had of them and acted accordingly. In other words, being thought of as beautiful made the women actually think of themselves as beautiful and exhibit "beauty" in their conversations.

Now, who hasn't walked a little taller or smiled a little brighter after being told how beautiful they look? But does the chameleon effect simply change our self-perception temporarily, or can it actually have long-term effects? New research from Yale indicates that diagnosis can indeed have a lasting effect on our health.

In Hartford, Connecticut, folks at a senior living center took a break from their regular activities to participate in a special hearing test administered by the Yale researchers. The seniors put on a pair of headphones that played a sequence of three ascending pitches for each ear. Each time the seniors heard a tone, they were supposed to raise their hand. Raise your hand after every tone and you get a perfect score of 6. Miss four of the six tones and you only earn a score of 2 out of 6, which means your hearing is fairly impaired. Given that everyone tested was over the age of seventy, it wasn't surprising that the average score was just 3.53.

Next the seniors were asked to perform a task that seemed completely unrelated to the hearing test. "When you think of an old person," they were asked, "what are the first five words or phrases that come to mind?"

The researchers noted how each person responded, and categorized each answer on two separate scales: one from very positive (e.g., "compassionate") to very negative (e.g., "feeble"), and another from external (e.g., "white hair") to internal (e.g., "experienced").

With two seemingly disparate sets of data—the hearing test and the attitude profile—in hand, the first phase of the study was complete. The hidden connection between the data was revealed three years later, when the same seniors were invited back to take the hearing test again.

Time had taken its toll, and, unsurprisingly, the average hearing score went down. But not all participants' hearing had deteriorated equally. Far worse off were those individuals who three years earlier had relied mostly on negative and external descriptors to describe old age. Even after statistically isolating the other factors that would diminish hearing (age, medical condition, etc.), the researchers found these external and negative perceptions of aging were responsible, on average, for a whopping 0.7-point drop in a person's hearing test score—the equivalent of the effect of eight years of normal aging alone—in just three years. In order to make sure that the senior citizens' self-diagnoses had affected hearing, and not the other way around, the researchers looked at those participants who had received a perfect score on the first hearing test. They found that among individuals who expressed negative and external stereotypes of old age, even those who had had perfect hearing scores the first time around were just as likely to experience diminished hearing as those who had started out with poor hearing.

Negative and external feelings about old age, in other words, can actually make people *physically* age faster. And the effect is not limited to hearing alone. Similar studies have found that negative stereotypes about aging contribute to memory loss and cardiovascular weakness, and even reduce overall life expectancy by an average of 7.5 years.

These studies reveal that psychology and physiology are inextricably connected in ways that no one imagined. To explore this dynamic more deeply, let's go to Capilano Canyon, a place whose beauty exemplifies the Pacific Northwest. Set against a mountainous backdrop, the area's lush old-growth rain forest is split by a dramatic canyon where the Capilano River flows. One of Vancouver's most renowned attractions, Capilano Canyon draws tourists and locals alike.

Nestled within these woods is a small but sturdy wooden bridge. Elevated ten feet off the ground, made of solid cedar, and bordered by guardrails, it offers a secure way across the stream.

A little farther up the canyon lies the Capilano suspension bridge. Built in 1889, this shaky rope structure spans 450 feet and hovers 230 feet above the ground. As wind blows down the canyon, the bridge sways, causing even the most sure-footed hikers to feel a little weak in the knees.

Little did the hikers taking in the scenery on one particular day know that the suspension bridge also had the power to sway their thinking.

At various times throughout the day, researchers had a young female assistant wait at the end of one bridge or the other. All the assistant knew about the research was that she was to adhere to a set of specific protocols. She was instructed to approach men between the ages of eighteen and thirty-five, one at a time, as they stepped off the end of each bridge. She would speak briefly to each man, following a scripted story—that she was a psychology student conducting a study on "the effects of exposure to scenic attractions on creative expression."

The assistant would then ask each man to fill out a short survey. When he was finished, she would offer to tell him about the study when she had a little bit more time. With that, she'd tear off a corner of the survey, jot down her name and number, and hand over the scrap of paper. Most of the men happily accepted the number and hiked off into the sunset.

The researchers also sent a young male assistant, armed with the same instructions, to approach men crossing each bridge. He gave the same spiel about a psychology study and likewise offered his telephone number should participants have any further questions. But unlike his female colleague, this assistant was repeatedly turned down by the subjects, who said "Thanks, but no thanks" to the offer. Over the next few days, only three curious guys called him up.

The female assistant's phone, on the other hand, started ringing right away and didn't stop. But what was interesting was *who* called her. Of the sixteen men who crossed the secure, wooden bridge, only two called. However, half of the eighteen men who crossed the suspension bridge called.

It's not likely that the men who called had developed a sudden interest in the psychology of creative expression. More likely, they had developed an interest in the psychology *assistant*. But had she miraculously become prettier or more attractive when talking to the men who crossed the suspension bridge? Why were those men so much more likely to call? The answer, the researchers concluded, was based on the relative shakiness of the two bridges.

Imagine walking across a rope bridge suspended hundreds of feet above a canyon. With each step, the bridge feels flimsier and less stable. You hold your breath; your heart rate increases; beads of sweat appear on your forehead. Physiologically speaking, the adrenaline rush you experience in such a situation is the same feeling of excitement you experience when you develop a crush on someone.

When the men who crossed the wooden bridge saw the research assistant, most of them looked at her and saw just that, a studious research assistant. But for the men who crossed the rope bridge, anxiety and adrenaline translated into a heightened romantic interest in the assistant. Their physiological reactions affected their perceptions. But could there be an alternative explanation? Could the nature of the bridges have acted as a filter of sorts, determining what type of men crossed them?

To test the possibility that the men who crossed the suspension bridge might simply be more courageous and daring than the group who crossed the wooden bridge, and thus more likely to take a chance on calling the assistant, the researchers went back to Capilano to conduct a follow-up study. In this second study, they stationed the female assistant only at the end of the suspension bridge. She approached some of the men right after they crossed; with others, before approaching them she waited for ten minutes after they had finished crossing. If the men who used the suspension bridge were indeed self-selecting brave souls, you'd expect both groups to call the assistant up in equal numbers, regardless of when she approached them. But the researchers confirmed the earlier results: the men who met the assistant when they had just crossed the bridge were much more likely to call than the ones who had been approached ten minutes later, when their anxiety had subsided and their adrenaline levels had gone down. The bridge's ability to enhance the men's romantic attraction earned it the moniker "the love bridge" within the psychological community.

We're constantly sending and receiving cues and subtle messages to and from one another—swaying and being swayed, even if our rational brain hasn't been let in on the secret. As these studies illustrate, we can't help but take on the characteristics others ascribe to us. There's a hidden dance at work within even the most seemingly straightforward interactions—and in this way, we're all psychological chameleons.

Chapter ⁶

In FRANCE, the SUN REVOLVES AROUND the EARTH

Who wants to trick a millionaire?

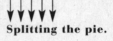

Splitting the pie.

Sentimental car dealers.

The talking cure for felons and venture capitalists.

Russian justice.

The rational Machiguenga.

ips puckered, Henri looked like he had just swallowed a spoonful of spoiled crème brûlée. He kept blinking, as if he could wish away the foul taste in his mouth. In the background, the music grew increasingly ominous.

The day had started out on an unusually hopeful note for Henri. Against the odds, he was selected from among thousands of hopefuls to be a participant in *Qui veut gagner des millions*, the French version of the game show *Who Wants to Be a Millionaire*. As Henri sat down in the tall chair onstage, the lights dimmed and host Jean-Pierre Foucault introduced the contestant and his girlfriend, Sophie, who was cheering him on from the audience.

Regardless of the country it's shot in, *Who Wants to Be a Millionaire* follows the same rules: contestants answer multiple-choice questions that grow progressively more difficult as the amount of money at stake increases. The first few questions are always gimmes, such as

Which family member did Red Riding Hood go and visit?
  A. Her mother
  B. Her sister
  C. Her grandmother
  D. Her second cousin, twice removed

They progress to more obscure trivia, such as "How many sailors accompanied Columbus on his voyage from Spain to the New World?" If contestants run into trouble, they can use one of three lifelines: call a friend for help, narrow down the answer choices, or poll the audience.

Henri had done well on the first few questions, but everything changed when the host asked him, "Qu'est-ce qui gravite autour de la terre?"—that is, "What revolves around the earth?"

Henri looked down in concentration as the answer choices were read aloud: (A) The moon, (B) The sun, (C) Mars, and (D) Venus. Henri reread the question out loud and mulled the choices over in his head. As the ominous music continued to play, he bit his lip. Seeing the contestant's puzzlement turn into genuine consternation, the host offered some advice: "Take your time, and if you have any doubts, use a lifeline."

Needing all the help he could get, Henri decided to invoke

his "ask the audience" lifeline. You'd think that Henri was smart to poll the audience. After all, even if some people get the answer wrong, in the aggregate the audience is usually right. But Henri was about to learn the hard way that our irrational perceptions of what's fair can dramatically sway our decision making.

"OK, audience, please use your answer pads," instructed the host. "Please answer this question for Henri . . . What revolves around the earth? If you know, please answer, and if you don't know, please abstain. (A) The moon, (B) The sun, (C) Mars, (D) Venus. You must vote now. Thank you!"

As the audience voted, the camera focused on Henri's girlfriend, dressed in a green sweater and fashionable red eyeglasses, looking utterly bewildered as to why her boyfriend couldn't come up with the right answer by himself. Then the camera panned across the French audience, capturing the dismay on their faces—a sign that they had made a diagnostic decision about Henri.

To say that Henri was no Galileo would be an understatement. Whether because he had slept through his elementary school science classes or because he was overcome with nervousness under the spotlight, Henri was stumped.

When the audience's answers were revealed, Henri took a deep breath, and swallowed hard: so much was on the line— he had to get this question right to stay in the game. As you might expect, no one in the audience voted for the answer that Venus revolved around the earth. For whatever reason, though, 2 percent voted for Mars. And then came the strange part. "If you allow me," said the host, "it is perhaps my own opinion, but the result is quite divided." Only 42 percent of the audience voted for the right answer, the moon. A full 56 percent voted for the sun revolving around the earth.

Henri was dumbfounded, and at this point we might ask whether something is horribly wrong with the French educational system. But it wasn't ignorance that the audience was exhibiting.

As we delve into what happened in France, we'll uncover our next psychological undercurrent—one that affects interactions from the boardroom to the jailhouse to the playground. It begins with a German experiment that anyone who had to share things as a kid can relate to. Researchers in Berlin placed a random pair of strangers in separate rooms. Each participant was told that he or she had been paired with a partner, whose identity would not be revealed. The pair would be given a combined sum of $10—but it was up to them to decide how to split it. The catch, though, was that the participants couldn't talk to each other, flip a coin, or enter into negotiation. Instead, one person was randomly chosen to decide how to split the money.

The splitting participant could divvy up the money any way he or she wanted. The receiving partner was then presented with the offer and had to decide whether to accept it or not. If the receiving partner accepted, both participants would collect their shares. If he or she rejected the offer, *both* parties would leave empty-handed.

This game would be played only once, so the participants

would be given no second chance. Furthermore, the participants were told that after the round was over, they would remain anonymous, going their separate ways.

Let's put ourselves for a moment in the shoes of the person deciding how to divvy up the sum. Most of us would probably opt to share the pot equally. Indeed, when it was time to make their choices, the majority of participants did decide to divide the sum right down the middle, so that each person would get $5. And all of the receiving partners who were presented with this offer accepted it.

The interesting part is what happened when the people deciding on the split gave themselves more than half. As you can imagine, their partners felt indignant. But were they indignant enough to walk away from the money? The answer, a vast majority of the time, was a resounding yes. Rather than accept the money that had been offered, most participants who were presented with an unfair split rejected it, opting instead to walk away empty-handed.

Now, from a purely rational perspective, it would have made sense for the receiving partners to accept *any* offer. After all, *some* money is better than *no* money. Two dollars, while not as good as five, is still better than zero. Regardless of the logic of such arguments, though, the overwhelming majority of partners who were presented with an unfair deal rejected the offer. They went home empty-handed but with the feeling that justice had been served.

What's more, their willingness to walk away from the deal when the split was uneven wasn't affected by the amount of money that was offered. When the same experiment was repeated with $100 instead of $10, participants were no more likely to accept an inequitable split.

What the study demonstrates is our deep-rooted belief in fairness and the great lengths to which we'll go to defend it. It was this adherence to the rules of fairness that swayed the French *Who Wants to Be a Millionaire* audience. Did Henri, who didn't know basic astronomy, really deserve a million euros? To the French audience, the answer—by a 56 percent to 42 percent vote—was a resounding no. They *deliberately* chose the wrong answer because it didn't seem fair to them for Henri to progress in the game with their help when he couldn't even answer such an easy question.

When Henri followed the audience's wrong answer, you could hear the spectators' muffled laughter. To them, giving the undeserving contestant the right answer would have been like allowing the uneven splitter to walk away with a disproportionate amount of money; it just wouldn't be fair.

But what if Henri had been someone the audience members expected less of—a first grader, for example? Would they have been as harsh? A variation of the "splitter" experiment sheds interesting light on this distinction. Participants in this study were presented with the same rules, except that instead of pairing up with another person, they were told they would be partnered with a computer, and that the computer would choose how to split the money. When the computer made "unfair" offers, the partners didn't balk. They were willing to accept an uneven split in the computer's favor, even though they would have rejected the same offer coming from a real person.

In other words, when it comes to fairness, it's the *process*, not the *outcome*, that causes us to react irrationally. This is called *procedural justice*. We don't expect a computer to be fair—but we do expect people to be.

Consider what would happen if we participated in a similar experiment where the person making the split was allowed to communicate with us. Imagine if he told us he was having financial difficulties and could really use the extra cash. We'd probably be willing to settle for less than half. Having been given a good reason for the inequitable split, we'd be less likely to feel that we were being taken advantage of and would be more likely to accept the offer.

But even the most calculating professionals are swayed by fairness. When you think of car dealers, you certainly wouldn't associate them with the notion of fairness. But despite their reputation for oily salesmanship and bilking consumers, in fact they're often the ones being taken to the cleaners—by auto manufacturers. Most car dealerships are relatively small operations and have little pricing power compared to the auto manufacturers. If you're a Ford dealer, for example, then Ford Motor Company is your only supplier; they control pricing and can dictate what your inventory will be. The dealers regularly pay high prices and get stuck with poor inventory—models that are difficult to sell but that the manufacturer needs to move.

When researchers talked to car dealers, they discovered

that the dealers evaluated their relationships with manufacturers in a surprisingly irrational way. A nationwide survey of car dealers revealed that rather than focusing solely on the results of their transactions with the manufacturers (Did I overpay? Did I receive high-quality inventory?), the dealers cared more about how the manufacturers *behaved* toward them. According to the research, what mattered to the dealers wasn't just whether they felt they got a good deal; they evaluated transactions by such seemingly insignificant details as whether the manufacturers "[took] pains to learn the local conditions under which dealers operate," acted in a "polite and well-mannered" fashion, and "treat[ed] dealers with respect." These fairness factors proved more important than the underlying economic numbers to the dealers' overall level of satisfaction with the outcome.

The researchers concluded that auto manufacturers and business managers alike "place too great an importance on margins and outcomes" when what was clearly more important to the customer was the perceived fairness of the process. They recommended that all managers—regardless of industry—put greater "effort, energy, investment, and patience" into nurturing the relationship. As the car dealer study suggests, how we are treated—the fairness of the procedure—has as much to do with our satisfaction as the ultimate outcome.

What is especially interesting about the issue of fairness is how important it is for people to feel they have a voice. A group of researchers asked hundreds of felons from Baltimore,

Detroit, and Phoenix to fill out a survey. These men had been convicted of crimes ranging from drug possession to fraud to armed robbery. The first part of the survey consisted of factual questions, such as the nature of their conviction and the length of their prison sentence. In part two, the survey moved on to questions about perceptions of fairness: How were you treated? How did you like the judge? Were the lawyers nice to you?

All of the survey questions fell into one of two categories: focusing either on the specific outcome—in this case a fine, probation, or prison time—or on how fair the process seemed—how the respondents perceived their journey through the legal system.

When researchers tabulated and analyzed the results, they found a peculiar pattern. As we'd expect, in evaluating the fairness of their trial, respondents placed a lot of weight on the outcome. Someone who got off with a light sentence naturally thought the trial was more fair than a guy who got the maximum sentence.

But it turns out that regardless of the crime they committed or the punishment they received, respondents placed nearly as much weight on the process as they did on the outcome.

One of the factors weighed most heavily by respondents was how much time their lawyer spent with them. The more time he or she spent with them, the more satisfied the respondents were with the ultimate outcome. Now, you'd think that the results would have been the opposite: a convicted felon who got stuck with a long sentence, especially after spending time with his attorney, would be angry. But it turns out that the behavior of his lawyer made a huge difference. In other words, although the outcome might be exactly the same, when we don't get to voice our concerns, we perceive the overall fairness of the experience quite differently.

The need to be heard, it turns out, isn't limited to just convicted felons. As you walk up Sand Hill Road in Menlo Park, California, with its modest-looking two-story office buildings, you don't notice anything particularly glitzy about the place. But on closer inspection, and after a couple of Ferraris go speeding by, you realize the affluence of the area. In these offices some of the nation's biggest high-tech companies had their start.

Sitting in their plush offices, venture capitalists in Silicon Valley and elsewhere around the country were asked about the entrepreneurial endeavors they had backed. Although the specific questions differed from those asked of the convicts, they fell into the same two general categories: outcome and process. The survey included specific questions about their dealings with entrepreneurs, such as "To what extent did the CEO provide you with timely feedback on the performance of the venture?" and "To what extent did the CEO keep you up to date on the performance of the venture?"

You'd expect the venture capitalists, or VCs, to be more analytical and detached in their reasoning than the felons. Simply put, a good investment is one that makes you money.

But when we look at the VCs' responses, it's clear that they, too, placed disproportionate weight on whether they felt their voices had been heard.

In analyzing the results, the researchers noticed that "timely feedback from an entrepreneur led investors to feel the entrepreneur was fairer, to trust the entrepreneur more, to be more supportive to the entrepreneur's strategic decisions, and to monitor the venture less frequently." If the investment's financial return is analogous to a prisoner's sentence—an objectively measurable result—the company's CEO is like the defense lawyer. A CEO who kept in touch gave the VCs a much more favorable impression of the underlying venture than did a CEO who was less communicative.

But this overemphasis on communication could be detrimental to a venture capitalist hoping to earn a good return on an investment. The VC-entrepreneur relationship is one in which it really *is* all about the money, and the frequency with which a CEO stays in touch with a VC has virtually no bearing on the success of the venture. A VC's evaluation of a venture should be only about the bottom line—how well the company is doing. For all he or she knows, the CEO who is uncommunicative might be the very one who is busy working night and day to help his start-up make it.

While the sway of procedural justice and our desire to have our voices heard are important to us all—whether we're car dealers, criminals, or venture capitalists—*how* we actually define fairness varies dramatically from culture to culture. Say that in the example of *Who Wants to Be a Millionaire* Henri changed his name to Henry and competed in front of an American audience. American audiences are almost certain to help out a contestant, regardless of his apparent abilities; data shows that in the United States, the "ask the audience" lifeline results in the correct answer more than 90 percent of the time.

When *Who Wants to Be a Millionaire* was introduced in Russia, though, the production team noticed that the audiences there would often give the wrong answer—and not just to confused souls like Henri. Russian audiences didn't discriminate—they deliberately misled both smart and less smart contestants alike. In fact, Russian audiences were so likely to give the wrong answer that contestants learned to be wary of the "ask the audience" lifeline.

When we contacted the *Who Wants to Be a Millionaire* production team for an explanation of the Russian phenomenon, they were just as perplexed. But Geoffrey Hosking, an expert in Russian history, had some interesting insights. We caught up with Hosking during his last week as a visiting professor at Princeton, as he was preparing to return to England, where he is on the faculty at University College London. Hosking first became fascinated with Russian culture during the time of Khrushchev; he is especially interested in why socialism was ultimately unsuccessful in Russia. Little did he ever imagine that his research would one day help explain the peculiarities of *Who Wants to Be a Millionaire.*

To solve the mystery of what prompted Russian audiences

to give wrong answers, Hosking took us back in time to peasant villages in the Russian countryside. Before the twentieth century, Hosking explained, peasant communities were governed by a principle of "joint responsibility." Everyone in the community acted together—whether paying taxes, supplying conscripts to the army, keeping peace in the community, or apprehending criminals. The peasants grew up expecting to lend one another a hand.

As the country became more industrial under the Soviet regime, people brought the old country ways to the city. Although life in communal Soviet apartments was cramped and difficult, Hosking explained, it was common for people to lend one another money and small items such as kitchen implements or matches. "It was fairly trivial stuff," he said, "and of course you find that a lot in other communities, not just Russian—but I think in Russia it was more systematic and expected." This attitude also prevailed at factories, where "Russians were constantly responsible for each other's lives."

But the same interdependent community that had your back could also turn against you if you stood out or were seen as different. In Hosking's view, this proclivity stemmed from the perception that "people who departed from the norm could be dangerous to the whole community—whether they were very rich or very poor. Either way, there was a tendency to seek the center and to resent people who were misfits."

And that, explained Hosking, is the key. "If people became very poor they were obviously a burden on the rest of the community. If they became rich it probably meant they were up to no good: they were criminals or did things which endangered the community."

This view of wealth is in direct opposition to Western attitudes toward wealth. "On the whole," Hosking reflected, "Americans regard it as justified if someone becomes rich. Now in Russia, the oligarchs"—a select group of entrepreneurs who found a way to make quick money after the Soviet collapse—"all achieved their wealth by means which were of dubious regard at best. That's the first thing that Russians resent. And secondly I think they resent the very fact that these people have become so much richer than everyone else."

From this perspective, it is clear that the *Who Wants to Be a Millionaire* audiences in Russia see contestants as trying to get rich on the backs of the audience members—and why should they contribute to such unfair behavior?

In their own ways, Henri and the Russian contestants violate a core pillar of their respective cultures' notions of fairness. What's fair in Moscow isn't necessarily fair in Paris or Berlin. As the world economy becomes more global, the differences between cultural interpretations of fairness become increasingly important.

Researcher Joseph Henrich decided to test the cultural universality of fairness. To begin with, Henrich replicated the money-splitting experiment among UCLA graduate students. He decided to use a dollar amount that he knew would be significant to students, and came up with $160, which translated to 2.3 days' worth of work at the grad students' standard university wage of $9 an hour. The rules of Henrich's experiment were exactly the same as those of the original study: you only play once, and you never find out who you were partnered up with.

As in the original study, the most common split offered in the UCLA study was 50/50, which the receiving partner always accepted. After the game was over, Henrich interviewed the participants to see what they had been thinking as they considered their offers. The same word came up again and again: fairness. "I thought that if I offered less than half," participants said, "my partner wouldn't accept the offer." And it turns out that the participants deciding on the split were right. Asked whether they would have accepted an 80/20 split—that is, an offer of $32—virtually all of the partners scoffed. "That would be unfair," they protested. They'd rather go home empty-handed. Some even went so far as to say that they would have categorically rejected *any* offer that was less than 50 percent.

Next, Henrich took his experiment on the road, heading to one of the most remote places on earth, deep into the Peruvian Amazon to visit the Machiguenga tribe. Eight hours from the nearest major city, the Machiguenga have been isolated from modern society for centuries. They live in small villages, but each family is self-sufficient, making its own tools and growing and gathering its own food.

Henrich brought along a translator who spoke a dialect of Arawakan, the native language. Next, he figured out what sum would be the equivalent of 2.3 days of work for the Machiguenga. Because the Machiguenga don't have their own currency, Henrich looked at what they earned from their occasional work for logging and oil companies that hired local labor. Their pay for 2.3 days of work came to twenty Peruvian soles.

Using that sum as the amount to be divided, Henrich carefully explained the rules of the game to the Machiguenga. But here in the Amazon, the game took a very different turn.

Unlike the UCLA participants—or, for that matter, participants from Japan, Indonesia, and Israel—the Machiguenga who made the split on average offered incredibly low sums to their partners. While the most common offer at UCLA was a 50/50 split, most Machiguenga offered an 85/15 split, favoring the person making the offer.

Even more strikingly, unlike the UCLA partners, who reacted to such lowball offers with indignation, when the Machiguenga partners were presented with these lopsided splits they nearly always chose to accept the offer. In so doing they were adhering remarkably closely to a rational economic model: from a purely objective, utilitarian perspective, it's logical to accept *any* offer rather than end up with nothing.

When interviewed afterward, the Machiguenga who accepted the offers laid out their reasoning. "Several individuals," explained Henrich, "made it clear that they would always accept any money, regardless of how much the proposer [splitter] was getting." Rather than viewing themselves as being treated unfairly by the offering partner, "they seemed to feel it was just bad luck that they were responders [choosers] and not proposers." The Machiguenga choosers viewed any offer as a generous gift. And those splitting the pie didn't see why they should give up half of their "winnings" to someone who was lucky just to get anything.

Some tribe members did make a 50/50 offer. When Henrich interviewed them, he found that each and every one of these people had spent significant time living among modern Westerners and felt the 50/50 split was the fair thing to do.

In the end, the Machiguenga are no more rational than are the UCLA students; they simply have a different perception of what's fair. In Russia it's not fair for one person to get rich. In America it's only fair if the splitter presents an even-steven offer. And in the Amazon jungle it's finders keepers.

We don't typically think of fairness as an irrational force, but it dramatically affects our perceptions and sways our thinking.

We've all been in situations where we had to negotiate a position. From an objective, logical perspective, it would make sense to focus strictly on the issue at hand: the offer we're presenting or the price we're asking for. But by talking through our reasons for that price or position, explaining how we arrived at it, and communicating what we feel is the fair thing to do, we can enjoy the same benefits as the attorneys who spent time with their clients and the entrepreneurs who talked frequently with their investors.

When we're busy completing a project at work, rather than assuming the final product speaks for itself, it's good to remember to regularly engage and update members of our team during the process. Similarly, when we travel to another country we should keep in mind that as we exchange currency, we also must shift our notions of fairness. As it turns out, because of these fairness sways, whether we're dealing with an auto dealer or a Machiguenga, it's not always true that what's fair is fair.

Chapter 7

COMPENSATION and COCAINE

Switzerland's toxic conundrum.

The GMAT rebels.

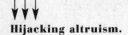

The power of the pleasure center.

Hijacking altruism.

Fast times at "Commie High."

The anticipation factor.

Whether they're Fortune 500 CEOs or high school principals, managers are always looking for ways to better motivate people. But is there a hidden side effect of bonuses and incentives meant to spur performance? What are the unintended consequences of offering people a financial carrot? To get a unique angle on the relationship between motivation and reward, let's travel to the University of Zurich, where researchers made some surprising findings.

Switzerland conjures up images of idyllic green pastures, snowy mountain ranges, and men in lederhosen blowing alpenhorns. The last thing that comes to mind is a mound of containers filled with toxic sludge.

In the 1940s, alarmed by the atrocities of World War II,

Switzerland's political leaders began developing a nuclear program. In typical Swiss fashion, the program priorities soon shifted to the more peaceful goal of creating nuclear power: five plants now provide about 40 percent of Switzerland's electricity. The country has a relatively clean energy program, but with any nuclear power comes nuclear waste—waste that has to go *somewhere*.

In 1993 the Swiss government identified two small towns as potential nuclear waste depositories, but they didn't know how the townspeople would react. Would they be outraged? Or, understanding the importance of the nation's nuclear energy program, would they "take one for the team"?

Two University of Zurich researchers were equally curious and decided to try to get some answers to this question. They asked the residents of the towns: "Suppose that the National Cooperative for the Storage of Radioactive Waste (NAGRA), after completing exploratory drilling, proposed to build the repository for low- and midlevel radioactive waste in your hometown. Federal experts examined this proposition, and the federal parliament decides to build the repository in your community." In a town hall meeting, the townspeople were asked whether they would accept this proposition or reject it.

Naturally, many people were frightened by the prospect of having the waste facility so close to their homes. But at the same time, whether out of social obligation, a feeling of national pride, or just a sense that it was the fair thing to do, 50.8 percent of respondents agreed to put themselves at risk for the common good. The other half of the respondents, however—those who said they would oppose the facility— still represented a significant obstacle for the government.

To see if this problem could be resolved, the researchers tested out a seemingly rational solution to bring the nuclear waste dump opponents on board. They talked to a new group of individuals from the same community and presented them with the same scenario, but added, "Moreover, the parliament decides to compensate all residents of the host community with 5,000 francs [about $2,175] per year and per person . . . financed by all taxpayers in Switzerland." Once again they were asked, in a town hall meeting, would they accept this proposition or reject it?

Now, from an economic perspective, a monetary incentive should make the proposition of living close to a nuclear waste storage facility easier to swallow. Indeed, we naturally assume that the best way to get someone to do something unpleasant or difficult is to offer some kind of financial incentive. It's why employers give bonuses when their employees take on more challenging or time-consuming work and why parents tie their children's allowances to performance of specific chores. Along this line of reasoning, the higher the compensation, the more likely it should be that people would do what you were paying them for.

Regardless of how much money is actually offered, though, rationally speaking, *any* amount of money should be better than nothing at all. That is, the $2,175 the Swiss researchers proposed might not be enough to convince *all* residents, but it should win over at least some of those who were opposed.

But that's not what happened.

For some reason, when the researchers introduced financial compensation into the equation, the percentage of people who said they would accept the proposition not only didn't increase—it *fell* by half. Instead of being motivated by the financial incentive, the townspeople were swayed to reject the nuclear dump en masse: only 24.6 percent of the people who were presented with the monetary offer agreed to have the nuclear dump close to their town (compared with the 50.8 percent who agreed when no money was offered). In addition to contradicting the laws of economic theory, this response just doesn't make sense.

Even when the researchers sweetened the deal to $4,350—and then again to $6,525—the locals remained firm in their opposition. Only a *single* respondent, in fact, changed his mind and accepted the offer when more money was put on the table.

Managers, parents, and, of course, economists have long operated under the assumption that monetary incentives increase motivation. But psychologists are beginning to discover that the connection between the two is trickier than it first appears. To understand what was really going on in Switzerland, we need to look into a paradoxical aspect of financial compensation, one that illuminates the strange relationship between monetary incentives and two very different parts of our brain.

Our first insight into this mysterious relationship can be found at an Israeli university where forty students sat with number 2 pencils in hand, preparing to take a mock version of the Graduate Management Aptitude Test (GMAT), the entrance exam used by most business schools.

Now, these Israeli students weren't actually applying to business school; they were taking the GMAT as part of a psychological study. Though they knew a high score on the mock test wouldn't result in admission to any MBA program, the volunteers were encouraged to do their best anyway.

Next the researchers brought in a separate group of forty students and asked them to complete the same test—but they added a concrete reward: for every right answer, a student would get 2.5 cents—not exactly enough to retire on, but better than nothing—which is what the first group of students received.

Check out the list of the actual student scores, ranked from highest to lowest. See if you can spot the surprising pattern.

Scores (out of a possible 50 points)

Students receiving no compensation	Students receiving 2.5 cents per correct answer
49	50
48	44
48	44
45	43
42	40

42	39
42	36
40	35
37	35
37	35
37	34
37	34
36	32
36	32
36	31
35	30
34	26
34	26
34	26
31	26
31	24
31	23
31	23
29	22
29	21
24	21
23	21
23	19
23	19
22	13
22	11
20	8
20	0

18	0
7	0
3	0
0	0
0	0
0	0
0	0

At first, the two columns look pretty similar. But the most interesting numbers are found down toward the bottom. Of the forty participants who weren't paid anything, four scored a zero on the test. Because the exam was multiple choice, getting a zero by dumb luck is virtually impossible. More likely, the four students simply thumbed their noses at the researchers. You pay me nothing, these rebels must have thought while filling the Scantron sheet with mockingly artistic designs, you get nothing in return.

But the group of paid participants had twice as many zeros. Now, you'd think that the opposite would be true: payment, after all, should act as an incentive to perform better. This is where the paradox witnessed in the Swiss countryside comes in. In each situation, the money effectively seemed to serve as a *dis*incentive: paid townspeople were *less* willing to host the dump, and compensated test takers *underperformed* on the exam.

When you look at the top 50 percent of performers in each group of test takers side by side, you see that the unpaid students *still* consistently beat out their paid counterparts, with an average score of 39 to the paid students' 34.9. In fact, looking across the board at all the scores, the students who didn't get a penny performed better than their paid counterparts, with an average score of 28.4, compared to the paid test takers' average of 23.1.

Economists can debate the reasons that such financial rewards backfire. But researchers at the National Institutes of Health (NIH) have been able to pinpoint the neurophysiology behind this paradox.

The NIH researchers placed participants in a specially modified MRI machine fitted with a computer monitor and a simple joystick. Lying inside the machine, the subjects played a video game reminiscent of the Atari era. At the start of each round of the game, either a circle, a square, or a triangle would appear on the screen. Each shape held a unique meaning. A circle meant that if you succeeded in completing an upcoming task—zapping a figure as it appeared on the screen—you'd earn a monetary reward. Different circles corresponded to different rewards. An empty circle was worth twenty cents. If the circle had a line through it, it meant that $1 was up for grabs; two lines meant a $5 reward.

When the subjects saw a square instead of a circle, they braced themselves for potentially bad news. The object of the game would be the same—zap the figure—except that *failing* to do so would result in a penalty of twenty cents, $1, or $5.

If the participants saw a triangle, it meant that no money

was on the line. Regardless of whether they hit the target or not, they would neither lose nor gain any money on that round.

While the participants were playing the game, they were shown a running tab of their earnings and losses. Meanwhile, the scientists monitored their brain activity. The scientists noticed that every time a circle or a square appeared—that is, every time there was money to be gained or lost—a certain part of the brain lit up. This region, which remained dormant when a triangle was shown (and no money was on the line), is called the *nucleus accumbens*.

The nucleus accumbens is, evolutionarily speaking, one of the most primitive parts of the brain, one that has traditionally been associated with our "wild side": it's the area of the brain that experiences the thrill of going out on a hot date, that sparks sports fans' exuberance when their team pulls out a last-minute victory, and that seeks out the excitement of Las Vegas. Scientists call this region the pleasure center because it is associated with the high that results from drugs, sex, and gambling.

At its most extreme, the pleasure center drives addiction. A drug like cocaine, for example, triggers the nucleus accumbens to release dopamine, which creates a feeling of contentment and ecstasy. The reason cocaine is so addictive is that the pleasure center goes into overdrive and the threshold for excitement climbs higher and higher. The MRI study surprised the researchers because it revealed that the pleasure center is also where we react to financial compensation.

And the more money there is on the line, the more the pleasure center lights up. A monetary reward is—biologically speaking—like a tiny line of cocaine.

Now, compare this reaction with our neurological reaction to altruistic behavior. In 2006, a few years after the NIH study, Duke scientists asked subjects to play a similar Atari-style video game, but instead of earning money for themselves, the participants were told that the better their score, the more money would be donated to charity.

In the MRI images, the pleasure center remained quiet throughout the game. But a completely different region of the brain, called the *posterior superior temporal sulcus,* kept lighting up. This is the same part of the brain responsible for social interactions—how we perceive others, how we relate, and how we form bonds. To make sure that the participants were reacting to altruism and not just to the act of playing a video game, they were also scanned while they watched a computer playing the game with the same charitable results. Despite the fact that the participants were just observers, the posterior superior temporal sulcus—what we'll call the "altruism center"—was hard at work.

Taken together, the findings of the Swiss nuclear depository survey and the Israeli GMAT study shed new light on the relationship between these two parts of the brain. Unlike, say, the parts of our brain that control movement and speech, the pleasure center and the altruism center cannot both function at the same time: either one or the other is in control. If the two brain centers functioned concurrently, then in the Swiss survey you would expect a compounding effect—that is, the percentage of townspeople who agreed to host the nuclear dump would have grown in accordance with the increase of the stipend. But that didn't happen. In the first half of the study—when no money was offered—the altruism center took charge, as people weighed the danger of having a nuclear dump nearby against the opportunity to help their country. The moment money was introduced, on the other hand, the entire situation got processed differently. The pleasure center took over, and in people's minds the choice came down to the dangers of the dump on one side and making a "quick franc" on the other. But the 5,000-franc stipend was much too low to excite the pleasure center.

The same thing happened with the GMAT takers. The moment monetary incentives were introduced, the altruistic motivation (completing the task to help out the researchers) waned, and money became the reason to proceed. But with such a small reward for the pleasure center, the students were more prone to slack off.

It's as if we have two "engines" running in our brains that can't operate simultaneously. We can approach a task either altruistically or from a self-interested perspective. The two different engines run on different fuels and also need different amounts of those fuels to fire up. It doesn't take much to fuel the altruism center: all you need is the sense that you're helping someone or making a positive impact. But the pleasure center seems to need a lot more—2.5 cents per right answer or a 5,000-franc stipend for agreeing to tolerate a nuclear dump site just isn't enough.

This intersection of economics, biology, and psychology regularly plays out in our everyday lives. Suppose a friend calls you and says he needs help moving. You might grumble a bit, but most of us would show up on a Saturday to help out. But what if your friend asked the same favor and offered to pay you $10 for your trouble? Chances are you'd decide that that small amount of cash wasn't worth a day of back-breaking labor, and you might remind your friend about the existence of *professional* movers. Likewise, imagine facing a deadline and desperately needing a coworker to stay until ten o'clock at night to help with the project. Your coworker would be more likely to stay late and pitch in if you explained your predicament and asked for a favor, rather than offering to pay her $15 for her time.

But it's about more than just simple favors. This finding should be of interest not only to those looking for help with an unpleasant task, but also to those running charities or holding fund-raisers. As anyone who has listened to an NPR or PBS pledge drive knows, not only are your donations rewarded with the knowledge that you're helping to keep public radio or TV in business, but you usually also score a free book, tote bag, or DVD in appreciation of your generosity. Yet the research we have been exploring suggests that this kind of payment may undermine our initial altruistic motivations.

It turns out that when the pleasure and altruism centers go head to head, the pleasure center seems to have the ability to hijack the altruism center. Let's take a look at how this neurological kidnapping plays out in a small magnet school in Michigan.

Community High School in Ann Arbor was founded in 1972 as the city's first alternative education school. The eclectic student body, combined with the school's unofficial mascot, the AntiZebra—a rainbow-colored creature who sported stars instead of stripes—earned the school the widely used nickname "Commie High."

From its inception, Community High was a place of few rules. Those that were in place—such as the mandatory wearing of shoes—were routinely overlooked. The high school had always been rich with opportunities for intellectual and creative freedom, and students were continually encouraged to develop their own unique strengths. As for the teachers, their starting salary in 1996 was $22,848. The disparity between a heavy workload and a low salary illustrates these professionals' dedication and commitment to helping students become well-rounded individuals. Indeed, Community High had a long waiting list to get in—new students literally had to line up for blocks in order to secure a spot in the school.

As the school's popularity soared, an opportunity arose to secure independence from the union and its regulations: a new state law allowed schools to operate more independently if they tried out new, innovative programs. And so, to gain this independence, Community High decided to start a pilot program. Although the faculty could not easily identify an urgent problem that needed solving, the school had to launch *some* new project. So, in true Community High fashion, the teachers and administrators convened and brainstormed.

In the course of their brainstorming the teachers recognized that students basically fell into two groups: those who were highly motivated and regularly came to class and those who were less enthusiastic and took advantage of the loose rules to skip classes. The goal of the pilot project would be to reverse the trend of skipping classes, improve overall attendance, and, in the process, increase student performance (the idea being that if you're not in school, it's difficult to learn). In order to evaluate attendance, on a random day in the last week of each semester teachers whose classes had at least 80 percent of their students in attendance would be rewarded with a salary bonus that equaled roughly 12 percent of their annual salary.

Now, remember, the school had adopted the attendance incentive merely as a way of implementing a pilot project requirement. Teachers had not demanded higher compensation, and Community High's attendance problems were not beyond the norm. Still, a few years into the program, the classroom inspections had shown that course completion had improved from 51 percent to 72 percent. The pilot seemed like an obvious success.

But a closer investigation revealed that the program was not as fruitful as it first appeared. For one thing, although the *completion* rate had gone up, the *attendance* rate had remained constant, falling just a tad from 59 percent to 58.62 percent. This means that although students were more likely to remain enrolled in a class, their attendance habits were no better than before the pilot study was launched. The most surprising finding, though, was what had happened to the average cumulative student GPA: it had taken a nosedive from 2.71 to 2.18.

During this period, academic standards at Community High hadn't changed, and the overall makeup of the student body remained the same. Moreover, GPA scores at a nearby school held steady over the same time period, indicating that the Community High figures were not simply part of a broader district trend. The decrease in average GPA pointed to a troubling conclusion: students weren't learning as much.

When researchers from the W. E. Upjohn Institute studied these figures and interviewed administrators and teachers, they gained an interesting insight. The researchers' analysis revealed that the teachers had shifted their focus. Once the pilot study was introduced, in order to secure their bonuses the teachers began concentrating their efforts on enticing students to show up who would otherwise have cut class. That is, rather than pulling a *Stand and Deliver* or a *Mr. Holland's Opus* and inspiring all students to achieve their true potential, the teachers followed a very different path.

Without anybody realizing it, the lure of a salary bonus

had pitted the teachers' pleasure centers against their altruism centers. All of a sudden the teachers had a bonus carrot dangling in front of them. Instead of focusing on teaching their students, they began chasing after the reward. To keep the students coming back to class they "included activities such as more field trips and in-class parties"—probably not what they had in mind when they entered the profession.

The Community High teachers didn't give up on their values or consciously lower their standards. It's just that the pleasure center has a way of sneaking up on us. Before we even know it, we've veered off the path we had originally planned. How does the pleasure center take over? Anton Souvorov, an economist at the University of Toulouse, has shown through an elaborate mathematical model that a reward can trigger an addictive response. Not only does our response to a monetary reward resemble our response to a drug like cocaine, but so does our drive to attain the reward. The Community High teachers exhibited the same types of behaviors as addicts seeking to get high, albeit to a much lesser extent: they became fixated on a reward and unknowingly altered their standards, goals, and conduct in the process.

Neuropsychologists have shown that activities associated with addictive substances and those associated with monetary rewards are both processed by the pleasure center. Because monetary incentives present such a strong allure to us, they distort our thinking. At Community High, what initially was created as a rational incentive program to increase productivity yielded out-of-character behavior with counter-productive results. Slowly but surely, the pleasure center overrode its altruistic counterpart.

Now, the problem isn't with rewards per se. It's only when you dangle the *possibility* of a reward ahead of time—creating a quid pro quo situation—that these destructive effects arise. An extensive review and analysis of motivation studies found that the prospect of a reward excites the pleasure center even more than the attainment of the reward itself. Taking a kid to Disneyland because she won the science fair is one thing, but telling her ahead of time, "If you enter the fair and win it, I'll take you to Disneyland," is another. It's that *anticipation* factor that drives the addictive behavior and suppresses the altruism center.

And it's true not just with children. Everywhere we look we see efforts to provide concrete financial incentives: from compensating star teachers whose students do well on standardized tests to giving tax credits to people who house Hurricane Katrina refugees. Of course, these individuals deserve recognition for their efforts. The problem with offering incentives, though, is that they carry a lot of baggage with them. For Swiss townspeople, Israeli students, and American high school teachers alike, throwing money into the mix diminished altruistic motivation and introduced unexpected behavior.

Chapter ⁸

DISSENTING JUSTICE

The Supreme Court conference.

Peer pressure and Coke-bottle glasses.

Ferris Bueller and the blocker.

"We are not focusing on the name you give to potatoes."

The captain is not God.

Not just thinking out loud.

Justice has been served.

Something strange happens when you put people in groups. They take on new roles, form "in group" alliances, get swept up by extreme stances, and succumb to peer pressure. In a group setting, the reasonableness of our thinking can be distorted and compromised. So it's not surprising that the hidden sways we have discussed so far reveal themselves just as prominently within a group setting. And nowhere are group dynamics more speculated about than within the marble walls of the highest court of the land.

The nine justices of the U.S. Supreme Court are aware that their every minute action and statement will be scrutinized—and amidst this scrutiny these lifetime appointees have to figure out a way of working together in the most efficient and productive manner. But just how exactly do group dynamics affect the decisions of the Supreme Court?

We spoke with Justice Stephen Breyer to better understand the procedures underlying the decision of a case. In talking to Breyer, what emerged was that the Court has found a way of circumventing a powerful psychological force that surfaces in nearly every group interaction.

To see how this happens, we'll look in on an important meeting called the "conference." This is the first time when all the justices convene in the same room to discuss the merits of the case before them. This conference is a justices-only meeting: no clerks, no audience, no outsiders.

But before we step inside, in order to get a true appreciation of the conference and just how much time and effort goes into the process of making a ruling, Breyer takes us back a few weeks, to the moment when a brief first lands on his desk.

The work starts with sifting through many different legal opinions. Breyer painted the picture: "First I get copies of briefs [memoranda] of maybe thirty to fifty pages each. And I usually have between ten and twenty briefs in a typical case." The briefs are submitted by the parties to the case and by supporters of one side or the other. As he reads each one, it's tough to remain neutral. "Now, all the time I have a very tentative hypothesis, but then I'm very open to being changed," he said. "I don't mind at all if I change, so I might go back and forth several times as I read it. I might read the government [brief] quite quickly because the government has good lawyers, and then I'll go through the amicus briefs. As I'm reading the briefs, I talk to my law clerks about them. Before the oral argument, I've read the brief, I've talked to my law clerk, my law clerk has written a memo, and then I have another conversation with my law clerk. And all that time I'm trying to make up my mind and I switch around and try different theories out." This back-and-forth process allows Breyer to distill all the information before formulating his stance. "And everyone [on the Court]," he noted, "has some process like that."

Once this is done, the justices are ready for the next stage, the week of oral arguments. The justices are not yet formally debating the case among themselves. "We hear the arguments and we're simply to ask questions," Breyer explained. "We ask questions of the parties—it's really not for them to make their argument at all; we already know their arguments. We're really asking questions about points that bother us."

Then it's time to start deciding the case. The justices may have shared memos with one another beforehand or talked informally, but the purpose here is to voice and discuss their opinions. By the time the conference convenes, the justices have had a chance to look at all sides, think the matter over, discuss troublesome points with their law clerks, query both sides, and hear their colleagues' questions.

The conference is purposely structured and has been run in essentially the same way since the 1800s. "In the conference, we go around the table in order of seniority, from the chief justice down to the most recent appointment," Breyer explained, "and everybody speaks once before anybody speaks twice." This ensures that every opinion is represented. "Each person might spend five minutes per case . . . They're trying to explain their reasons for which direction they're leaning. And everybody writes down what everybody else says. And then there'll be some discussion back and forth afterwards. And on the basis of that discussion—which is a preliminary discussion—it's fairly clear how the Court is likely to break down."

The group dynamic that the conference unintentionally avoids was first empirically studied by Solomon Asch in a landmark psychology experiment. This study not only illuminates what goes on in the Supreme Court, but also explains how the role played by a single individual can shift an entire group's opinion.

In Asch's study each participant was placed in a room with several other people. The participants were told they would be tested for visual acuity. The task seemed simple enough: the group was shown three straight lines of varying lengths, and each person was asked to determine which of the three lines matched a fourth line. It was pretty straightforward; the lengths were so glaringly different that you certainly didn't need a magnifying glass or a ruler.

But what the participant didn't know was that the other "subjects" in the room were really actors, and all of them had been instructed to give the same wrong answer. As the actors called out their erroneous answers one by one, the real participant was bewildered. But something strange happened: rather than stick to their guns, most participants began to doubt themselves and their lone dissenting opinion. What if I misunderstood something, or what if I've been looking at the lines from a weird angle? Time and again, they figured that it was best to go along with the group—and save themselves the embarrassment of being odd man out. Indeed, 75 percent of subjects joined the group in giving the wrong answer in at least one round.

Now, it's easy to dismiss the study participants as being too easily manipulated. But regardless of how independent-minded and steadfast we may think we are, we're all tempted at times to align ourselves with a group. We may worry that if we voice an unpopular viewpoint others will doubt our intelligence, taste, or competence. Or we may just not want to make waves. The challenge is to know when to speak up.

Breyer explained that even when the thought "Oh, I'm the only one" arises, he'll speak up, saying something like, "I actually don't agree, but I'll swallow it because there's no point writing a dissent in this. I don't feel *that* strongly about it." He added, "If I'm all by myself, I have to feel pretty strongly before I write a dissent." This reasoning makes perfect sense. If justices were to write a formal dissent every time they disagreed on a small point, the Court would come to a standstill. But the fact that a dissenter speaks up can make all the difference.

As Asch found, although the sway of group conformity is incredibly strong, it depends on unanimity for its power. In a variation of the line study, Asch ran the experiment exactly as before (an unsuspecting participant, a room full of actors giving the wrong answer), but this time he added a single actor who gave the right answer. This lone dissenting voice was enough to break the spell, as it "gave permission" to the real participant to break ranks with the other members of the group. In almost all cases, when a dissenter spoke up, the participant flew in the face of the group and gave the correct response. The really interesting thing, though, is that the dissenting actor didn't even need to give the *right* answer to inspire the real participant to speak up with the correct response; all it took to break the sway was for someone to give an answer that was *different* from the majority.

To prove how powerful the dissenter—even an incompetent one—really is, a clever experiment was conducted. In this variation, administered by psychologist Vernon Allen, a participant was once again placed in a group made up of actors and asked to answer simple questions. But in this version each participant was told that before the start of the study he would have to fill out a self-assessment survey alone in a small office. After five minutes, a researcher knocked on the door and told the participant that due to a shortage of rooms, he would have to share the space with another subject (who was in reality—you guessed it—a paid actor).

The most striking thing about the actor was the eyeglasses he wore. As Allen details in the study, the glasses were custom-made by a local optometrist and fitted "with extremely thick lenses that distorted the wearer's eyes, and gave the impression of severely limited visual ability." In this case, "extremely thick" is an understatement: the lenses were so Coke-bottle-like that they had to be ground down in the middle "to allow enough normal central vision to prevent the confederate's experiencing headache and eyestrain."

As if that weren't enough, to really drive home the point of the actor's "visual impairment," the actor and a researcher engaged in a pre-scripted conversation. "Excuse me, but does this test require long-distance vision?" the actor asked apologetically. When the researcher affirmed that yes, it did, the actor explained, "I have very limited eyesight"—as if that were a surprise to anyone—"and I can only see up-close objects." Showing concern, the experimenter asked the actor to read an easily legible sign on the wall. After straining and squinting to make out the words, the actor, alas, failed. Point made.

The researcher explained that he needed all five people for the study, claiming the testing apparatus did not work with fewer than five subjects. He invited the actor to participate, stating, "Just sit in anyway, as long as you are here. Since you won't be able to see the questions, answer any way you want; randomly, maybe. I won't record your answers."

But the actor, thick glasses and all, still enabled participants to escape from the sway of the group. Ninety-seven percent of participants conformed to the group when there was no dissenter present, but only 64 percent conformed when the visually impaired confederate was among them giving a different—but equally wrong—answer. Obviously, we wouldn't expect a clearly incompetent dissenter to turn around as many participants as would a competent dissenter, but it's important to note that the presence of a dissenter—any dissenter, no matter how incompetent—still made it possible for a large segment of participants to deviate from the majority and give the right answer.

The power of the dissenter, as we'll soon see, plays out not only in the Supreme Court, but also in international diplomacy and airline safety. But before we see how, it's important to understand the full power of the psychological dynamics underlying this force. To do so, we turn to a family therapist. David Kantor, a Boston-based family therapist, led what might very well have been the first incarnation of reality TV. In an effort to study how schizophrenia manifests in family systems, Kantor set up cameras in various rooms of people's houses, then pored over hours of footage of ordinary folks' lives. Although Kantor's research didn't tell him much about schizophrenia, he did detect a pattern that emerged again and again within every group dynamic, regardless of whether schizophrenia was a factor.

In analyzing the tapes of the families he studied, Kantor found that family members traded off playing the same four distinct roles. The first role was that of the *initiator*: the person who always has ideas, likes to start projects, and advocates for new ways of moving forward. Think of someone like Matthew Broderick's character, Ferris Bueller, in *Ferris Bueller's Day Off.* The entire movie is about Ferris's new, creative ideas for something fun to do: let's ditch school, take a vintage car out for a joyride, sneak into a fancy restaurant, attend a baseball game, and star in a parade while we're at it. When you're in the same room with a Ferris Bueller type, it's hard not to get excited about whatever new project or idea he has in mind. You can always count on initiators to come up with new ideas; they aren't necessarily the life of the party, but they're definitely the ones who suggest having a party in the first place.

If initiators are represented by Ferris Bueller, their opposites—*blockers*—are like Ferris's friend Cameron. Ferris wants to take a joyride; Cameron is afraid of getting caught. Ferris wants to go to a nice lunch; Cameron points out that they don't have a reservation. Whatever new idea the initiator comes up with, the blocker finds fault with it. "Let's go to Disneyland!" exclaims the initiator. "No, it's too expensive," retorts the blocker. "Let's start a new company!" "Most fail within the first year." If hanging out with Ferris Bueller makes us want to go out and do something fun, spending a minute with Cameron makes us reluctant to do anything. Of course, it's easy to think of blockers as pure curmudgeons. But as we'll soon see, they play a vital role in maintaining balance within a group.

Initiators and blockers are bound to lock horns, which is when the *supporter* steps in, taking one side or the other. If there's a decision to be made, you can bet on the supporter siding with either the initiator or the blocker. The fourth role, that of the *observer*, stays fairly neutral and tends to merely comment on what's going on: "It seems we're having a disagreement about whether or not to go to Disneyland."

Most of the tension in the group lies between the initiator and the blocker. Initiators are all about making new things happen. They have a wealth of fresh ideas. They might be wildly optimistic and have a tendency to rush to action, but their creativity, energy, and drive can be instrumental when it comes to innovation. In contrast, blockers question the merit or wisdom of new decisions. Instead of merrily going along for the ride, they raise points about the potential harmful consequences that might follow.

It's easy to see why people and organizations are naturally attracted to initiators. They bring in fresh energy and new ideas, and for them the sky is always the limit. It's equally easy to see why those same people and organizations would want to steer clear of blockers.

Think of how American politicians and media, for example, reacted to the French during the days leading up to the second Iraq war. At the time, taking on the role of initiator, the U.S. administration made countless arguments to convince politicians and foreign nations to join America in war. White House personnel motivated, energized, and pushed forward—and, before long, managed to get public opinion on their side.

But when the president tried to get a UN resolution passed in support of the war in Iraq, French foreign minister Dominique de Villepin tried to block the measure, firmly announcing, "We will not allow a resolution to pass that authorizes resorting to force." Likewise, when Bush wanted to push forward and go in to search for weapons of mass destruction, President Jacques Chirac decreed "total confidence" in the UN inspectors doing the job without further intervention. And when the United States was getting ready to attack, de Villepin warned instead about "the North Korean regime . . . It's in no way better than Iraq's and has weapons of mass destruction, in particular nuclear ones which aren't hypothetical, but, regrettably, definitely exist."

The French were quickly branded as obstructionists, and Congress got so upset that it actually passed a resolution officially renaming the Capitol cafeteria's french fries "freedom fries." In true blocker fashion, the French embassy retorted, "We are at a very serious moment dealing with very serious issues, and we are not focusing on the name you give to potatoes."

Now, the French made an argument that—in retrospect—should have merited more careful attention. But because they so conveniently fit the role of the blocker, the French were simply seen as a thorn in Bush's side.

As tempting as it is to dismiss them, though, blockers do, in fact, play a vital role in maintaining balance in a group. A blocker functions as the brakes that prevent the group from going down a potentially disastrous path. Even if the blocker's opinion is wrong, at least it adds a perspective to the debate—giving others an opportunity to look at things in a different light.

Breyer explained how the role of the blocker serves a necessary function in the Supreme Court: "If somebody is going to write a dissent . . . they have a point, they have some kind of point they're trying to make. Quite often the opinion [of the majority] is changed somewhat in response to comments and opinions [of the dissenters]. Occasionally—maybe once or twice a year—the whole Court shifts."

Even when dissenters don't have enough votes to change the Court's opinion, they still affect the process. "It makes the other person take account of the point. They have to answer it or they have to take it into account," Breyer said.

"Last year," Breyer recalled, "I disagreed very strongly in this case involving segregation or desegregation or affirmative action. How did I show I was feeling so strongly? I wrote a seventy-seven-page dissent—which I never do. Never. The longest I had previously written was probably about twenty pages. So that was unusual, and then I spoke for twenty minutes from the bench, which was *very* unusual, and I knew it was unusual. So there are structured ways of saying if you think that there's something that's wrong."

Although Breyer knew that the Court was unlikely to change its mind, by voicing his views he put his arguments on the record, forced other justices to respond to them, and provided a springboard for Congress to create new laws.

There's no question that dissenters in a group setting do make the process messier, and blockers are not always given much of a voice. "In many European countries," explained Breyer, courts "don't publish dissenting opinions. [Judges] can disagree, but they only have one opinion, because they want people to think that the law is what it is—no argument with it. It's true in Belgium; it's true in the EU."

It's easy to understand the desire to present a unified front. But as Breyer pointed out, the end result—in this case, the Supreme Court's majority opinion—is actually improved by dissent. "The thing about writing a dissent," Breyer reflected, "is it's actually a pain in the neck for the person who is writing the [majority] opinion . . . and suddenly [has] to deal with this dissent." The majority has to revise its opinion in response to points raised by the dissenters, then the dissenters rebut, and on and on it goes. As Breyer put it, "People keep writing and writing and writing." But the process serves an important function. "How is that helping? Well, it's helping because it makes it a better opinion. Because people [justices] have to think through all the rejections."

As Breyer pointed out, "People have different views on this. Some people, like [former Chief Justice] Rehnquist, thought it was a waste of time to dissent. He didn't like to dissent. And sometimes he hardly bothered to answer a dissent. Other people, like Justice Scalia, they'll answer. They don't like anything to go out with an argument on the other side that hasn't been answered."

Blocking might not be pleasant—for anyone involved— but it's a necessary component of healthy group dynamics— one that can literally save lives.

Think back to Captain Van Zanten's decision to take off from Tenerife airport without tower clearance. The accident that occurred sent shockwaves through the aviation world. In the aftermath of the crash, agencies scrutinized cockpit recordings from every plane crash and near miss over the years. Seventy percent were determined to be the result of human error, and the majority of those errors had to do with team dynamics. Listen, for instance, to the final seconds of the cockpit recording of Van Zanten's flight.

When Van Zanten put his hand on the throttle and revved up the engines, the first officer instinctively tried to stop him: "Wait a minute. We don't have ATC clearance."

Van Zanten agreed, but seemed irritated at the attempt to thwart or delay him. "I know that," he responded. "Go ahead and ask."

What's striking is that the copilot starts to dissent but is immediately rebuffed. Indeed, when Van Zanten tries for the second time to take off, the first officer keeps quiet. And without the voice of the blocker, a deadly sequence of events unfolds.

NASA's research into plane crashes ultimately helped revolutionize aeronautical procedures. A new model for cockpit interaction was born: Crew Resource Management (CRM), which teaches pilots, among other skills, how to be effective blockers. We interviewed Dr. Barbara Kanki, a psychologist who was recruited by NASA to work on CRM at the Ames Research Center because of her expertise in nonverbal communications. "I knew nothing about aviation, space, or the military," Kanki reflected about her early days working for NASA.

But her expertise fit right in with NASA's effort to improve airline safety. "Up till then," Kanki explained, the standard explanations for crashes relied on physical causes. "You had a plane crash because something broke or the pilot flew into the mountain—not exploring what was underneath the problem." The question of *how* a crew ended up in such disastrous situations intrigued Kanki. When researchers evaluated pilot performance on a mission simulation, according to Kanki, they found that "performance differences did not seem to be tied to technical skills. It seemed more to do with management skills. And that was the turning point."

Thanks to researchers like Kanki, the aviation field has been transformed. Looking back at the pre-Tenerife years, Southwest Airlines captain Lex Brockington explained, "In the airline industry there was a time when the captain was almighty, in charge of everything, almost godlike. The captain was making a decision and everyone else was scared to overrule him and wouldn't open their mouths."

Van Zanten was a celebrated captain. Not only would questioning his judgment have been embarrassing, it would have been tantamount to mutiny. How could you criticize a call made by the head of safety at KLM?

But CRM has changed these dynamics. "When I came into Southwest Airlines," Brockington explained, "there was a big push to get around these human-error mistakes. CRM is distinctly designed to get away from that 'the captain is the man' view. Now, the captain is still ultimately in charge of the airplane. But nowadays it's not like the captain is God.

Even when pilots interview for a job, they give them scenarios and they tell them, there's a first officer next to you, the dispatch (the person who puts together all the paperwork and flight planning), and so on." Pilots are trained to communicate effectively and accept feedback, and crew members are taught to speak up when they see that their superior officer is about to make a mistake.

Captain Brockington likes to take it even a step further. "I like to vocalize my thoughts. I think out loud. That way the person sitting next to me always knows what I'm thinking. And if the copilot can detect a flaw in my thought pattern, he or she is more apt to speak up. They don't say you have to do that, but I think it's a good idea."

Brockington gave us a case in point. "Let's say you're cruising along and you have a lot of thunderstorms out there, you've got weather building up, you're heading to a certain airfield, and you're getting close enough to actually see some of these storms develop or the radar points them out. Now you're thinking, 'Hey, I've got weather building up. I'm looking at the wind; it looks like it's moving in that direction. If it gets that way, we're going to start looking at the weather, find some other alternate bases we can go to. If we have to hold in a holding pattern, do we have enough gas?'"

Because the presence of a strong initiator can quell a blocker, Brockington consciously takes on the role of an observer. "Now, I can sit there and not say anything," he explained, "and all of a sudden we go into holding patterns and the first officer knows nothing about what I'm doing. I just made the decision and off we went, versus saying exactly what I said to you." Brockington's method of thinking out loud makes it easier for the first officer to weigh in with a different point of view or challenge the captain when necessary.

At Southwest, they really push this culture of teamwork. "We only hire people who are very friendly and outgoing people," Brockington said. The crew and officers stay at the same hotel and socialize together, as well. "We invite the crew to come down. If you feel the captain is approachable, you're certainly more apt to speak up if you have a concern." Brockington tells his crew, "We all make mistakes, so I really want you to speak up if you have a problem. If you see something that you don't like, it won't hurt my feelings."

When Brockington goes in for his annual CRM course, one of the instructors he might get is Captain Cathy Dees. She teaches CRM to new hires and a refresher course for current Southwest pilots. When pilots spot a departure from safety procedures, they are *trained* to challenge the captain. The challenge takes the form of three steps that all Southwest pilots know by heart. "The first step," Dees said, "is to state the facts"—for example, "Our approach speed is off." If that's ineffective, the next step is to "challenge." According to Dees, research has shown that "generally the best way to challenge someone is to use their first name and add a quantifier to the fact. 'Mike, are you going to make it on this approach? Check your altitude.'" That will get the captain's attention and bring him or her out of the tunnel vision he or she may be experiencing. "It's important to state the fact without being condescending," she said.

If these two procedures fail, the third step is to "take action. If someone were flying an unstable approach—that means they were approaching the runway and they were perhaps a little too high or too fast, or not in a condition to make a normal landing—we would want them to go around," Dees explained. The action Dees advises would be to get on the radio and say, for example, " 'Southwest 1 going around, we're too high.' And once you say something on the radio, the tower controller will cancel your landing clearance. And that way the action takes place without physically fighting over equipment in the airplane, which might aggravate the person flying."

More often than not, the first two steps are enough to get a captain's attention; there is rarely a need for the first officer to take action. The training emphasizes the need for the blocker to speak up and for the person in charge to listen and communicate effectively.

This freedom to give feedback and voice concerns—and the willingness of those in charge to tolerate dissent—is just as important in a boardroom, where a costly mistake can be averted by being open to dissent from blockers in the group. Accordingly, it's not just pilots who have benefited from CRM training. The medical community is also responding to human-error failures by adapting aviation's approach to crew coordination. The Agency for Healthcare Research and Quality is supporting research at the University of Texas to apply aviation safety practices and training concepts to medicine, particularly in operating rooms and emergency rooms.

CRM training is also being used in industrial settings, such as offshore drilling operations and nuclear power plants. The training helps workers in control rooms and emergency command centers avoid making operational errors that could lead to accidents.

Whatever the situation, be it the cockpit or the conference room, a dissenting voice can seem, well, annoying. And yet, as frustrating as it can be to encounter blockers, their opinions are absolutely essential to keeping groups balanced. It's natural to want to dismiss a blocker's naysaying, but as we've seen, a dissenting voice—even an incompetent one—can often act as the dam that holds back a flood of irrational behavior.

Epilogue

Swimming with the riptide.

The power of the long view.

Zen economics.

Propositional thinking.

One man's trash is one woman's masterpiece.

A cable guy, a banker, and a pharmaceutical rep.

The real devil's advocate.

Perched above the beach, a tube of sunscreen in one hand and a whistle in the other, lifeguards are trained to watch out for the greatest danger associated with swimming in the ocean. The cause of 80 percent of near drownings, this threat isn't clearly visible at first glance; instead it lurks unseen.

When underwater sandbars form near the shore, they act as dams, keeping water from flowing back to the ocean. The pressure builds, ultimately breaking the sandbar and creating a rip current as the water pours through the breach. Anyone unfortunate enough to be in the riptide's path will be dragged away from the shore.

One's natural reaction, of course, is to try to swim *against* the current and back toward the beach. But even strong swimmers are no match for the current's force. As any lifeguard can tell you, the best way to escape the pull of a riptide is to swim parallel to the shore until you escape the current's path.

Similarly, when it comes to psychological undercurrents, the best way to counter them isn't necessarily to follow our natural instincts. That's what makes avoiding these invisible forces so challenging—sometimes it's our instincts that cause us to be swayed in the first place.

But there are antidotes that we can use to avoid getting carried away by these currents. Our quest for a way to overcome our irrational aversion to loss led us back to Jordan Walters, the financial adviser from Smith Barney. Jordan offered an example that illuminates his perspective on overcoming this psychological force: "Let's say you're traveling on a long trip and you have a flat tire," Jordan began. After fixing the tire, you have two choices: you can look for shortcuts to make up the lost time and completely rearrange your trip, or you can continue on your way and accept that you're running behind schedule. Jordan advocates the latter, "longview" method: You might be a little late, but "you're on your way again and you still know where you're going." Rearranging your trip on the fly, on the other hand, can get you thoroughly lost.

When things go wrong, we can either apply a short-term, Band-Aid solution or remember that in the grand scheme of things it's only a minor misstep. Having a long-term plan—and not casting it aside—is the key to dealing with our fear of loss.

"Our clients," explained Jordan, "are really in it for long-term capital accumulation and preservation." The challenge is not to allow short-term fluctuations—a "flat tire," if you will—to get in the way of one's long-term plan.

The same is true in our everyday lives. "You won't believe what just happened to me," our friend Erin recently told us. The day before, we had talked to her about our findings on loss aversion, about how it skews and distorts our thinking and judgment. She told us she had been sitting in her car on a congested street in San Francisco. "This idiot in front of me," she complained, "wouldn't move. The light turned green, and he just sat there." Without even thinking about it, Erin had her foot on the gas pedal, ready to swerve into the oncoming traffic lane to pass the guy. But just as she was about to carry out the maneuver, she thought of what we had told her about Jordan. "I realized I was being loss averse, trying to avoid losing time, and I thought, 'What am I doing?'" Instead of reacting to a short-term impulse (trying to save a few seconds), she took a long-term view (realizing that those few seconds weren't worth putting her life in danger).

Our natural tendency to avoid the pain of loss is most likely to distort our thinking when we place too much importance on short-term goals. When we adopt the long view, on the other hand, immediate potential losses don't seem as menacing.

Seeing firsthand how powerful and detrimental snap judgments can be, Jordan decided to teach his kids the value of long-term thinking. "I created an investment game," he told us, "that looks at the longer term." Jordan was reacting to the way in which schools introduce children to investing. "If you look at the schools and their investment games, the difficulty is that they have to work with a semester: a short time horizon. So you're given a certain amount of hypothetical money, you pick a few companies, see who wins at the end of a few months. But there's a problem with that in that you're looking at a very short-term window rather than at a full market cycle. You're looking at a market that could melt in three months or surge in three months, and you really haven't looked at the company's fundamentals. So what I did is take away the time barriers."

Jordan spent time with his children helping them evaluate companies in sectors they would be familiar with—toy manufacturers, food makers, restaurant chains—and purchase select stocks. But his focus was not so much on which companies they chose as on the time horizon involved. And how often do Jordan's kids check the prices of their stocks? "They follow the stocks on an annual basis," he says. Once a year—looooooong term.

If looking far into the future is the way to avoid the faulty decision making that can result from loss aversion, the antidote to getting swept up in commitment—the force that keeps us from giving up on a project even though it's clearly failing—is to don Zen Buddhist glasses and learn to let go of the past. There's a point where we have to accept that what's done is done, and it's better to shift direction than to dig ourselves deeper into a hole.

The "letting go of the past" strategy holds true whether you're a government official financing a dead-end public works project—because so much has already been invested in it—or a marketing manager continuing to support a failed campaign because you don't want to be seen as a quitter. It just doesn't make rational sense to stay aboard a sinking ship. As one venture capitalist told us about managing investment expectations, "Sometimes you just have to know when to shoot it in the head."

In his book *Only the Paranoid Survive*, Andy Grove, former CEO of Intel, tells the story of how in 1985 he and Intel cofounder Gordon Moore decided to get out of the memory chip business and focus all their resources on the emerging field of microprocessors. At the time, their core business was memory chips. As Grove explained, "Our priorities were formed by our identity; after all, memories *were* us." But Intel had been losing money on memory chips for some time, as a result of the entry of high-quality, low-priced, mass-produced Japanese chips. Clearly, Intel needed to do something. Grove related, "I was in my office with Intel's chairman and CEO, Gordon Moore, and we were discussing our quandary. Our mood was downbeat. I looked out the window at the Ferris wheel of the Great America amusement park revolving in the distance, then I turned back to Gordon and I asked, 'If we got kicked out and the board brought in a new CEO, what do you think he would do?' Gordon answered without hesitation. 'He would get us out of memories.' I stared at him, numb, then said, 'Why shouldn't you and I walk out the door, come back, and do it ourselves?' " That was how Intel overcame the sway of commitment and made its momentous decision to concentrate on microprocessors, paving the way for the company to become one of the greatest success stories in American business.

When we find ourselves unsure about whether or not to continue a particular approach, it's useful to ask, "If I were just arriving on the scene and were given the choice to either jump into this project as it stands now or pass on it, would I choose to jump in?" If the answer is no, then chances are we've been swayed by the hidden force of commitment. Making a clean break might feel uncomfortable, but it could be in our best interest.

Avoiding the next stream also requires a Zen-like approach. The best strategy for dealing with the distorted thinking that can result from value attribution is to be mindful and observe things for what they are, not just for what they appear to be. You have to be prepared to accept that your initial impressions might be wrong.

Simply realizing that we're making judgments based on assumptions about a situation or a person's value can free us from this sway. Remember the SoBe experiment, where people who drank the cheapo SoBe performed worse on a mental acuity test than did those who drank a full-priced version of the exact same drink? In a variation of that study the researchers ran the experiment as before, but this time they asked the participants before the test whether they thought the price they had been charged for the drink would affect their concentration. Now, if the answers to these questions seem obvious, that's the point. The researchers wanted the participants to think about the fact that the price of the drink had nothing to do with its potency. Indeed, those students who received the cheapo SoBe *and* had to answer this question experienced no decrease in their mental acuity scores, performing just as well as their counterparts who received the full-priced drink.

In similar fashion, Elizabeth Gibson had to fight her natural inclination toward value attribution when she was walking down a street on Manhattan's Upper West Side and spied a piece of art wedged between two garbage bags. She was tempted to walk away, but then she stopped to reflect about the art. "I had a real debate with myself," Gibson told the *New York Times*. "I almost left it there," she said. "It was so overpowering, yet it had a cheap frame." So Gibson took it home, where she hung it on her wall. Years later she discovered the true provenance of the painting. Known as *Tres Personajes*, it had been painted by renowned Mexican artist Rufino Tamayo. The painting had been stolen and later discarded. Had Gibson come along twenty minutes later, it would have already been picked up by the garbage collectors. Instead, the painting was auctioned by Sotheby's for over a million dollars. Had any of the other pedestrians who passed by known that this piece belonged in a museum, they would certainly have snatched it up. Instead, they evaluated it by its surroundings and cheap-looking frame and passed it by.

Whether we're shopping at a clearance outlet or a chic boutique, we sometimes need to fight our tendency to consciously dismiss an item because of its price. Instead, we should ask ourselves, "If I got this item as a gift, would I like it? If it cost $1—or $1,000—how would my perception of it shift?" The more we become aware of the factors affecting the perceived value of a person or object, the less likely we are to be swayed by value attribution.

But not all sways are so easily vanquished. It's virtually impossible for us not to make judgments about people and situations. We judge, or diagnose, the world around us (and, in turn, get diagnosed) all the time. In the case of job interviews, we can reduce our tendency toward the diagnosis bias by instituting regimented structures that force us to focus on objective data. But what about instances where we can't follow a script or we don't have access to hard data? Is there a practical way to reduce the bias that comes with diagnosis?

Psychologist Franz Epting suggests that we can overcome our tendency to succumb to the diagnosis bias through what's called "personal construct theory." One of the main principles of this theory is that we make diagnostic errors when we narrow down our field of possibilities and zero in on a single interpretation of a situation or person. All of us have certain lenses, or constructs, that we use to sift through the endless flow of information we encounter. For example, when we meet new people we may judge them on whether they dress well or poorly, whether their shoes are polished or not, whether they seem to be liberal or conservative, whether they are religious or secular, hip or nerdy. These constructs are useful insofar as they help us to quickly assess a situation and form a temporary hypothesis about how to react. Forming initial opinions is one of the ways in which we try to make sense of the world given limited time or information. But we have to be careful not to rely too much on such preemptive judgments, as they can short-circuit a more nuanced evaluation. They can narrow our perceptions and make us more apt to get swayed by a hasty diagnosis.

What personal construct theory teaches us is to remain flexible and examine things from different perspectives. Epting explained that this approach is called "propositional thinking." It's all about keeping evaluations tentative instead of certain, learning to be comfortable with complex, sometimes contradictory information, and taking your time and considering things from different angles before coming to a conclusion. It can be as straightforward as coming up with a kind of self-imposed "waiting period" before making a diagnostic judgment.

When it comes to the fairness sway, our emotional reaction can be just as intractable and difficult to set aside. One way to counter the fairness sway is to try to weigh things objectively and not succumb to emotional maneuvers or moral judgments (Would I rather achieve my goals or teach the other person a lesson?). But what can we do in situations where our actions are being evaluated based on how fair others perceive them to be?

One answer comes from research conducted at Duke University. The results of the study sound like the beginning of a bad joke: What do a cable guy, a banker, and a pharmaceutical representative have in common? Researcher Jack Greenberg studied how employees from these different sectors perceived their performance evaluations. He found that regardless of the industry, it was incredibly important for employees to feel that they were active participants in the evaluation process. The employees were more likely to feel that the process was fair when supervisors solicited their input prior to an evaluation and used it during the process; when there was two-way communication during the evaluation interview; and when the employees had the chance to challenge or rebut an evaluation. In other words, if the employees were *involved* in their evaluation, they felt it was fairer. Another study found the same to be true of employees' perceptions of pay raise decisions.

When we make decisions or take actions that will affect others, keeping them involved will help ensure that they feel the process is fair. It's important to keep others apprised of our decision-making process—to communicate what we're thinking: "I know this is a tricky situation; I'm not sure what to do myself. I think the best course of action is to do such-and-such." Voicing our own discomfort or uncertainty shifts the focus to the situation at hand. A potentially divisive situation can be transformed into a collaborative effort, allowing people to evaluate the facts objectively, rather than be swayed by the sense that the process was unfair.

Just as communicating our process is important, so is giving voice to the dissenter. In group situations, the presence of a blocker can actually make the decision-making process more rational and less likely to go off the tracks. It gives us a new appreciation for someone who tends to play "devil's advocate." The term originated in the Vatican to refer to a priest designated to argue against a papal nominee. The priest assigned to represent the devil's position, so to speak, brought balance to the debate. Although no one is likely to win a popularity contest by playing the devil's advocate, businesses would do well to respect a dissenting opinion—if not straight-out encourage someone to take on such a role. The dissenter, of course, is as likely to be wrong as anybody else, but the discussion of the points made by the dissenter can add perspective to the debate.

Living in a time when we can predict hurricanes, treat diseases with complex medical interventions, map the universe, and reap the benefits of systematized business approaches, it's easy to forget that under the surface we humans are still influenced by irrational psychological forces that can undermine a logical perspective on the world around us. The fact is, all of us are swayed at times by factors that have nothing to do with logic or reason. From NBA coaches to heads of state, from managers looking to hire a job applicant to trained psychiatrists studying why we act the way we do, each of us brings a variety of different experiences, emotions, and perceptions to our thinking. It is only by recognizing and understanding the hidden world of sways that we can hope to weaken their influence and curb their power over our thinking and our lives.

Acknowledgments

When Liz Hazelton moved to Doubleday, we could only hope that fate would reunite us. Liz's dedication, spirit, and enthusiasm are unparalleled, and we couldn't have asked for a better team at Currency/Doubleday. We're grateful to Roger Scholl for his editorial expertise, commitment to excellence, and continual direction and encouragement; Sarah Rainone for her thoughtful feedback, fresh ideas, and unwavering support through the process; Talia Krohn for her editorial contributions; Michael Palgon for his strategic thinking; Nicole Dewey for nailing the subtitle; Meredith McGinnis for her endless supply of creative ideas; and Louise Quayle for her hard work on our behalf.

This book wouldn't have materialized without the continual support of our fantastic agent, Jennifer Gates. We're grateful for the invaluable advice we received from Esmond Harmsworth and Mary Beth Chappell, as well as for Rachel Sussman's pinch-hitting.

Thanks to Larry Leson for being the best speaking agent we could ask for and for making the finest gazpacho in the world.

Speaking of the finest, this book wouldn't have sounded half as good without Hilary Roberts, and we wouldn't have looked half as good without Josyn Herce.

We're indebted to the many experts who shared their stories, knowledge, and experience with us: Justice Stephen Breyer for his thoughtful reflections; Steve Spurrier for taking time out during spring training (and Rita Ricard for arranging the interview); Jordan Walters for his sage advice; Dan Ariely for his insights and ideas; Franz Epting for providing clarity and wisdom; Dean Falk for her precision and passion; Bruce Wampold for his articulate explanations; Lex Brockington for his view from the helm of a 737; Cathy Dees for her enlightening explanations; Barbara Kanki for her informative history of CRM; Allen Huffcutt for his sharp and entertaining analyses; Marco Gemignani for his views on cultural dynamics; Becca Levy for discussing her research with us; Eric Johnson for helping us navigate the economic waters; David Antonuccio for illuminating a complex subject; Geoffrey Hosking for offering cultural insights; Adele Barker for her fascinating stories; Max Bazerman for his helpful insights; Saar Gur for his venture capitalist perspective; Toni Vaughn Heineman for her enthusiasm and passion; Tammy Johns and Mara Swan for their wisdom about hiring practices; "Dr. Hastings" and the other physicians we spoke with for providing a fascinating window into the medical world; Shani Harmon for illuminating Kantor's group roles; and Alex Olhovich for inspiring new ideas.

We're also grateful to all the people who have supported us through this process: Denise Egri (wielder of the red pencil); Auren Hoffman (don); Noah Kagan (initiator); Dina Kaplan (New York catalyst); Juliette Powell (power diva); Pete Sims (author/thinker); Michael Breyer (courtroom connector); Josh Rosenblum (intellectual at large); Andreea Nicoara (genius/translator); Noah Brier (marketing guru); Sara Olsen (cheerleader); Dave Wallack (strategist); Dave Blatte (monk); Marc Blatte (novelist); Jeanne Neary (shiksa goddess); Marianne Manilov (organizer extraordinaire); John and Alison Roberts (editors/proofreaders); the ESi crew (WebEOCers); Cort Worthington (creative counsel); René Wong (advertising genius/El Paso holdout); Pablo Pazmino (doctor/human rights student activist); Pam and Roy Webb (critical thinkers); Mark Schlosberg (do-gooder); Matt Miller (scientific adviser); the Lischinsky family (sounding boards); Kyle Bach (consigliere); and Mom and Dad (parents).

Thanks also to musician Jason Kleinberg for providing the fiddle music on our Web site, and to John Hoffsis and Craig Sakowitz for lending their voices. New York accommodations provided by Corey Modeste and Peter Fleischer.

Notes

Preface

The names of the medical doctors and patients in this section have been changed.

Chapter 1

10 **The passengers aboard KLM Flight 4805:** Macarthur Job and Matthew Tesch describe the chain of events leading up to the Tenerife air collision in *Air Disasters: Volume 1* (Fyshwick, Australia: Aerospace Publications, 1994), pages 165–80. PBS's *NOVA* program "The Deadliest Plane Crash" offers a documentary perspective on the disaster. Information about the *NOVA* episode, as well as a link to the cockpit recorder transcript, can be found at http://www.pbs.org/wgbh/nova/planecrash.

17 **egg sales in southern California:** Daniel Putler's egg study, "Incorporating Reference Price Effects into a Theory of Consumer Choice," was published in *Marketing Science* 11 (1992): 287–309.

Notes

You may need to refresh your calculus and advanced economics theory before reading Putler's study, as it is geared to the academic reader and contains advanced mathematical formulas and graphs.

19 **orange juice shoppers in Indiana:** The orange juice study that replicated Putler's egg findings, "Modeling Loss Aversion and Reference Dependence Effects on Brand Choice," was authored by Bruce Hardie, Eric Johnson, and Peter Fader and published in *Marketing Science* 12 (1993): 378–94. We found *Advances in Behavioral Economics*, edited by Colin Camerer, George Loewenstein, and Matthew Rabin (New York: Russel Sage Foundation, 2004), to be a great source for examples of loss aversion, including the egg and orange juice studies.

19 **when we sign up for a new phone service:** "Mental Accounting Matters" by Richard Thaler (chapter 3 of Camerer, Loewenstein, and Rabin, eds., *Advances in Behavioral Economics*) describes telephone customers' preference for a flat-rate fee—including a reference to Kenneth Train Press's *Optimal Regulation* (Cambridge, Mass.: MIT, 1991), p. 211—and contains a footnote about the AOL flat-rate-pricing chain of events.

20 **AOL stumbled upon this same phenomenon:** The interview with AOL CEO Steve Case about the flat-rate-pricing shift appeared in the *Washington Post* on December 9, 1997. The article is titled "A Conversation with Stephen M. Case, CEO of America Online."

22 **Jordan Walters:** All identifying client details in the Jordan Walters interview have been changed to preserve client anonymity.

Chapter 2

30 **"twenty-dollar auction":** Information about Max Bazerman's auction of a $20 bill can be found in his book *Judgment in Managerial Decision Making* (New York: John Wiley & Sons, 2002), pages 79–80. When we talked to Bazerman, we learned that he now

188

performs a $100 version of the auction for executives. This auction goes up in $5 increments. But the higher stakes don't prevent enthusiastic bidding. Bazerman originally got the idea for the auction from Martin Shubik's "The Dollar Auction Game: A Paradox in Noncooperative Behavior and Escalation," which can be found in the *Journal of Conflict Resolution* 15 (1971): 109–11.

33 **LBJ was surely the hands-down winner:** We found helpful information about LBJ in Robert Dallek's *Flawed Giant: Lyndon Johnson and His Times, 1961–1973* (New York: Oxford University Press, 1999); and Doris Kearns Goodwin's *Lyndon Johnson and the American Dream* (New York: Harper & Row, 1976). All LBJ quotes in this chapter were taken from his public speeches, recorded conversations he had with his staff, or information he provided to his biographer, Doris Kearns Goodwin.

37 **George W. Bush's remarks about Iraq:** All George W. Bush quotes are taken from public speeches he gave during his presidency.

38 **Nobel Prize–winning economist Daniel Kahneman:** Daniel Kahneman and Jonathan Renshon applied behavioral economic dynamics to politics and war in their article "Why Hawks Win," published in the January/February 2007 issue of *Foreign Policy*. The article can be found in its entirety at http://www.foreignpolicy.com/story/cms.php?story_id=3660.

Chapter 3

42 **Dr. Dean Falk, an anthropology professor and forensic expert:** Our knowledge of *Homo floresiensis*, the evolutionary island effect, Brodmann area 10, and the anthropological disputes about the discovery came from an interview with Dr. Dean Falk.

45 **a precocious young Dutch student named Eugene Dubois:** You can learn more about Eugene Dubois from Pat Shipman's *The*

Man Who Found the Missing Link (New York: Simon & Schuster, 2001).

49 journey beneath the streets of Washington, D.C.: You can read more about Joshua Bell's performance in the Washington, D.C., metro station in Gene Weingarten's article, "Pearls Before Breakfast," which appeared in the *Washington Post* on April 8, 2007. The article and a video segment of the performance are available at http://www.washingtonpost.com/wp-dyn/content/article/2007/04/04/AR2007040401721.html.

52 that is, until Charles Dawson came along: The Piltdown hoax is detailed in several books, including John Evangelist Walsh's *Unraveling Piltdown* (New York: Random House, 1996).

55 a clever experiment using SoBe Adrenaline Rush: The SoBe study was conducted by Baba Shiv, Ziv Carmon, and Dan Ariely. Titled "Placebo Effects of Marketing Actions: Consumers May Get What They Pay For," it was published in the *Journal of Marketing Research* 42 (2005): 383–93.

57 Ohio State theater department's productions: We learned of the Ohio State University discounted theater ticket phenomenon from "The Psychology of Sunk Cost," by Hal Arkes and Catherine Blumer, published in *Organizational Behavior and Human Decision Processes* 35 (1985): 124–40.

62 modern anthropologists from universities and museums: The scientific debate surrounding *Homo floresiensis* has continued to unfold since our interview with Dr. Falk. In September 2007 a new study analyzing the wrist bones of the Hobbit revealed that they are different and distinct from human bone structures, cementing the likelihood that *Homo floresiensis* is indeed its own separate—and fascinating—species. To learn more about the studies investigating *Homo floresiensis*, see D. Falk, C. Hildebolt, K. Smith, M. J. Morwood, T. Sutikna, P. Brown, Jatmiko, E. W. Saptomo,

B. Brunsden, and F. Prior, "The Brain of LB1, *Homo floresiensis*," *Science* 308 (2005): 242–45; D. Falk, C. Hildebolt, K. Smith, M. J. Morwood, T. Sutikna, Jatmiko, E. W. Saptomo, B. Brunsden, and F. Prior, "Response to Comment on "The Brain of LB1, *Homo floresiensis*," *Science* 312 (2006): 999; T. Jacob, E. Indriati, R. P. Soejono, K. Hsu, D. W. Frayer, R. B. Eckhardt, A. J. Kuperavage, A. Thorne, and M. Henneberg, "Pygmoid Australomelanesian *Homo sapiens* Skeletal Remains from Liang Bua, Flores: Population Affinities and Pathological Abnormalities," *Proceedings of the National Academy of Sciences* 103 (2006): 13421–26; Z. Laron, L. Kornreich, and I. Hershkovitz, "For Debate: Did the Small-Bodied Hominids from Flores (Indonesia) Suffer from a Molecular Defect in the Growth Hormone Receptor Gene (Laron Syndrome)?" *Pediatric Endocrinology Reviews* 3 (2006): 345–46; M. Tocheri, C. Orr, S. G. Larson, T. Sutikna, Jatmiko, E. W. Saptomo, R. A. Due, T. Djubiantono, M. J. Morwood, and W. L. Jungers, "The Primitive Wrist of *Homo floresiensis* and Its Implications for Hominin Evolution," *Science* 317 (2007): 1743–45.

Chapter 4

68 **Buried within this mountain of data:** The NBA draft order study was authored by Barry M. Staw and Ha Hoang. The researchers used an empirical methodology called *factor analysis* to analyze players' statistics and distill the data into three distinct categories of related elements: quickness, toughness, and scoring. They then ran a regression analysis to evaluate the significance of draft order picks on a player's career. The study was published in *Administrative Science Quarterly* 40 (1995): 474–94.

71 **the students of Economics 70:** Harold H. Kelley of the University of Michigan authored the experiment about the "warm"

professor. It is titled "The Warm-Cold Variable in First Impression of Persons" and published in the *Journal of Personality* 18, no. 4 (1950): 431–39.

75 **Professor Allen Huffcutt:** We interviewed Allen Huffcutt of Bradley University about his knowledge and research relating to employment interviews. He is currently working on a new research-based conceptual model with colleagues Phil Roth and John Kammeyer-Mueller that attempts to improve our understanding of, among other things, how a candidate's performance shapes interview decisions.

77 **daydreaming about their girlfriend or boyfriend:** Tara K. MacDonald and Michael Ross conducted the college freshman dating experiment. It is titled "Assessing the Accuracy of Predictions About Dating Relationships: How and Why Do Lovers' Predictions Differ from Those Made by Observers?" and was published in *Personality and Social Psychology Bulletin* 25 (1999): 1417–29.

84 **in South Africa when a consumer lending bank:** The data about the bank loan offer variables is described in a June 17, 2005, working paper titled "What's Psychology Worth? A Field Experiment in the Consumer Credit Market," by Marianne Bertrand, Dean Karlan, Sendhil Mullainathan, Eldar Shafir, and Jonathan Zinman. It is available at http://www.princeton.edu/~rpds/downloads/Shafir_2006What's%20Psych%20Worth_%20South%20Africa.pdf.

Chapter 5

90 **It had the makings of an epidemic:** The analysis of the data that revealed the fortyfold increase in bipolar diagnoses is found in "National Trends in the Outpatient Diagnosis and Treatment of Bipolar Disorder in Youth," by Carmen Moreno, Gonzalo Laje, Carlos Blanco, Huiping Jiang, Andrew Schmidt, and Mark Olfson. It

was published in the *Archives of General Psychiatry* 64 (2007): 1032–69.

92 **a psychiatrist named Emil Kraepelin:** Information about Emil Kraepelin's methodology and deviation from scientific protocol can be found in Michael Shepherd's "The Two Faces of Emil Kraepelin," published in the *British Journal of Psychiatry* 167 (1995): 174–83.

93 **pharmaceutical companies increasingly began to draw attention:** Dr. David Healy's article "The Latest Mania: Selling Bipolar Disorder" provides an overview of the events leading to the exponential increase in the diagnosis of bipolar disorder. It was published in *PLoS Medicine* 3 (2006): 185. It can be viewed in its entirety at http://www.pubmedcentral.nih.gov/articlerender.fcgi?tool=pubmed&pubmedid=16597178.

94 **who believes in empirical, quantitative evidence:** Bruce Wampold's research about the factors responsible for effective psychotherapy is presented in his book *The Great Psychotherapy Debate: Models, Methods, and Findings* (Mahwah, NJ: Lawrence Erlbaum Associates, 2001). In the book, Wampold compares the medical model of therapy with what he calls the *contextual model* and shows that the vast majority of the assumptions underlying the medical model are not empirically supported. Because Wampold's research underscores the importance of the client-clinician working relationship, he encourages prospective clients to seek a competent practitioner with whom they feel comfortable and whose therapeutic style and approach match their preferences.

97 **sugar pills and Prozac had about the same therapeutic effect:** As part of our investigation into the bipolar diagnosis and the medical model, we spoke with Dr. David Antonuccio, professor of psychiatry and behavioral sciences at the University of Nevada. Antonuccio and two of his colleagues, David Burns and William

Danton, reviewed studies that examined the effectiveness of SSRI antidepressant drugs, and they authored an article titled "Antidepressants: A Triumph of Marketing Over Science?" It was published in the electronic journal *Prevention and Treatment* 5 (2002), available at http://www.antidepressantsfacts.com/2002-07-15-Antonuccio-therapy-vs-med.htm. One of the meta-analytical studies they examined analyzed FDA data on clinical drug trials. This study, titled "The Emperor's New Drugs: An Analysis of Antidepressant Medication Data Submitted to the U.S. Food and Drug Administration," was written by Irving Kirsch, Thomas Moore, Alan Scoboria, and Sarah Nicholls. It was published in the electronic journal *Prevention and Treatment* 5 (2002).

97 **The would-be commanders didn't know:** Dov Eden and Abraham Shani wrote about the army officers' diagnoses of their trainees and the reciprocal effect that followed in "Pygmalion Goes to Boot Camp: Expectancy, Leadership, and Trainee Performance." It was published in the *Journal of Applied Psychology* 67 (1982): 194–99.

99 **A meta-analysis conducted by psychologists at SUNY Albany:** A meta-analysis conducted by Nicole Kierein and Michael Gold found that managers' perceptions of their workers influence productivity levels. The study, titled "Pygmalion in Work Organizations: A Meta-Analysis," was published in the *Journal of Organizational Behavior* 21 (2000): 913–28.

101 **fifty-one women waiting for the phone to ring:** The study about the women who were perceived as sounding beautiful is titled "Social Perception and Interpersonal Behavior: On the Self-Fulfilling Nature of Social Stereotypes." It was authored by Mark Snyder, Elizabeth Decker Tank, and Ellen Bercheid and published in the *Journal of Personality and Social Psychology* 35 (1977): 656–66.

104 **New research from Yale:** "Hearing Decline Predicted by

Elders' Stereotypes," authored by Becca Levy, Martin Slade, and Thomas Gill, was published in the *Journal of Gerontology: Psychological Sciences* 61B (2006): 82–88.

105 **And the effect is not limited to hearing alone:** Becca Levy has published articles about aging and longevity ("Longevity Increased by Positive Self-Perceptions of Aging," by Becca Levy, Martin Slade, Suzanne Kunkel, and Stanislav Kasl, published in the *Journal of Personality and Social Psychology* 83 [2002]: 261–70); functional health ("Longitudinal Benefit of Positive Self-Perceptions of Aging on Functional Health," by Becca Levy, Martin Slade, and Stanislav Kasl, published in the *Journal of Gerontology: Psychological Sciences* 56B [2002]: 409–17); and improved memory ("Improving Memory in Old Age Through Implicit Self-Stereotypes," by Becca Levy, published in the *Journal of Personality and Social Psychology* 71 [1996]: 1092–1107).

106 **the Capilano suspension bridge:** To learn more about the research involving the young men who misinterpreted their feelings toward a research assistant, see "Attraction Under Conditions of High Anxiety," by Donald Dutton and Arthur Aron. It was published in the *Journal of Personality and Social Psychology* 30 (1974): 510–17.

Chapter 6

115 **The pair would be given a combined sum of $10:** The pioneering study examining the roles of the two players in the ultimatum games was authored by Werner Guth, Rolf Schmittberger, and Bernd Swarze. Titled "An Experimental Analysis of Ultimatum Bargaining," the study was published in the *Journal of Economic Behavior and Organization* 3 (1982): 367–88.

118 **When you think of car dealers:** "The Effects of Supplier Fairness on Vulnerable Resellers" was written by Nirmalya Kumar,

Lisa Scheer, and Jan-Benedict Steenkamp. It was published in the *Journal of Marketing Research* 32 (1995): 54–65.

120 **A group of researchers asked hundreds of felons:** The study about procedural fairness and convicted felons, titled "Procedural Justice in Felony Cases," is by Jonathan Casper, Tom Tyler, and Bonnie Fisher. It was published in *Law and Society Review* 22 (1988): 483–508.

121 **Sitting in their plush offices, venture capitalists:** The venture capitalist study, titled "Procedural Justice in Entrepreneur-Investor Relations," is by Harry Sapienza and M. Audrey Korsgaard. It was published in the *Academy of Management Journal* 39 (1996): 544–74.

123 **Geoffrey Hosking, an expert in Russian history:** Geoffrey Hosking has authored numerous books about the Russian people and their history, including *Russia and the Russians: A History* (Cambridge, Mass.: Belknap Press, 2003); and *Rulers and Victims: The Russians in the Soviet Union* (Cambridge, Mass.: Belknap Press, 2006).

In learning about Russian culture, we had the pleasure of interviewing Dr. Adele Barker, a professor at the University of Arizona and editor of *Consuming Russia: Popular Culture, Sex, and Society Since Gorbachev* (Durham, NC: Duke University Press, 1999). She told us the following story, which exemplifies the cultural contrast between Western values and life during the Soviet era: "It was the middle of winter, like minus a million degrees. I was sitting on a bus, and across from me was a little old lady, and I looked at her and then a couple of minutes later I looked at her again and I smiled. And she didn't smile back, but it wasn't unusual. And when she got up to get off, she came up to me and she said in Russian—I'll never forget it—'Young lady,' she said, 'here we do not smile.' And it meant two things: one, there's nothing to smile about, but two, you don't know me and I don't know you and we don't do that. We don't do that. Because you don't know with whom you're having business, as they say in Russian. There isn't the same sort of chattiness with strangers in Russia as there is in the States."

125 **the differences between cultural interpretations of fairness:** Joseph Henrich's study about the Machiguenga is found in "Does Culture Matter in Economic Behavior? Ultimatum Game Bargaining Among the Machiguenga of the Peruvian Amazon," published in the *American Economic Review* 90 (2000): 973–79.

Chapter 7

133 **Two University of Zurich researchers were equally curious:** The Swiss nuclear incentive study, titled "The Cost of Price Incentives: An Empirical Analysis of Motivation Crowding-Out," was conducted by Bruno S. Frey and Felix Oberholzer-Gee. It was published in the *American Economic Review* 87 (1997): 746–55.

136 **forty students sat with number 2 pencils:** The GMAT study conducted in Haifa, Israel, can be found in Uri Gneezy and Aldo Rustichini's "Pay Enough or Don't Pay at All," published in the *Quarterly Journal of Economics* 115 (2000): 791–810.

139 **to pinpoint the neurophysiology behind this paradox:** Brian Knutson is one of the pioneers of neuroeconomics, an emerging field that investigates the various regions of the brain associated with decision making. You can read about the role of the nucleus accumbens in "Anticipation of Increasing Monetary Reward Selectively Recruits Nucleus Accumbens," by Brian Knutson, Charles Adams, Grace Fong, and Daniel Hommer. The study was published in the *Journal of Neuroscience* 21 (2001): 1–5.

141 **our neurological reaction to altruistic behavior:** The study exploring the neurological aspects of altruism is titled "Altruism Is

Associated with an Increased Neural Response to Agency." It was conducted by Dharol Tankersley, Jill Stowe, and Scott A. Huettel and published in *Nature Neuroscience* 10 (2007): 150–51.

144 **a small magnet school in Michigan:** To find out more about the results of the pilot study conducted at Community High School, see "Teacher Performance Incentives and Student Outcomes," by Randall Eberts, Kevin Hollenbeck, and Joe Stone, published in the *Journal of Human Resources* 37 (2002): 913–27.

147 **a reward can trigger an addictive response:** The economics paper suggesting that rewards are addictive, "Addiction to Rewards," was written in 2003 by Anton Souvorov at the University of Toulouse.

148 **It's only when you dangle the *possibility:*** The meta-analysis study suggesting that rewards interfere with intrinsic motivation when they are presented in a quid pro quo fashion is titled "Extrinsic Rewards and Intrinsic Motivation in Education: Reconsidered Once Again." Authored by Edward L. Deci, Richard Koestner, and Richard M. Ryan, it was published in *Review of Educational Research* 71 (2001): 1–27.

Chapter 8

153 **In Asch's study:** Solomon Asch's classic study about the pressure to conform to a group was published in *Groups, Leadership, and Men,* edited by Harold Guetzkow (Pittsburgh: Carnegie Press, 1951). Asch's chapter, titled "Effects of Group Pressure upon the Modification and Distortion of Judgment," appears on pages 177–90.

154 **it depends on unanimity for its power:** Asch's study about the freeing effect of a dissenter is titled "Opinions and Social Pressure." It was published in *Scientific American* 193 (1955): 31–35.

155 **the dissenter—even an incompetent one:** Vernon Allen and John Levine conducted the study featuring the visually im-

paired actor. Their study is titled "Social Support and Conformity: The Role of Independent Assessment of Reality." It was published in the *Journal of Experimental Social Psychology* 7 (1971): 48–58.

163 **NASA's research into plane crashes:** Barbara Kanki, who works for NASA Ames, is the coeditor (together with Earl Wiener and Robert Helmreich) of *Cockpit Resource Management* (San Diego: Academic Press, 1995), a resource book that describes the application, philosophy, and history of CRM.

Epilogue

172 **sitting in her car on a congested street:** Our fast-driving friend "Erin" (a.k.a. Speedy Gonzales) asked that her real identity be concealed; she was afraid that this book could be used against her if she ever gets into an accident. We hope she continues to heed Jordan Walters's advice and reforms her driving habits.

179 **The results of the study sound like the beginning of a bad joke:** To learn more about how fairness operates in the workplace, read "Determinants of Perceived Fairness of Performance Evaluations," by Jerald Greenberg, published in the *Journal of Applied Psychology* 71 (1986): 340–42.

You can also read "Effects of Procedural and Distributive Justice on Reactions to Pay Raise Decisions," by Robert Folger and Mary Konovsky, published in the *Academy of Management Journal* 32 (1989): 115–30.

Index

Addiction, 140, 147, 148

Aging, negative stereotypes about, 104–5

Allen, Vernon, 155–56

Altruism-pleasure conflict, 140–48

Anticipation factor, 148

Antonuccio, David, 97, 193–94n

AOL, 20

Ariely, Dan, 56

Asch, Solomon, 153, 154–55

Asymmetric reactions, 18

Attendance incentive experiment, 144–48

Barker, Adele, 196–97n

Barkley, Charles, 66

Bazerman, Max, 30–32, 188–89n

Bell, Joshua, 49–50, 57

Bipolar disorder epidemic, 90–94, 96–97

Bowie, Sam, 67

Brain functioning, 139–44

Breyer, Stephen, 151–53, 154, 161–62

Bridge-crossing experiment, 106–9

Brockington, Lex, 164–66

Bush, George W., 37–38, 160

Car dealers, 118–19

Chameleon effect

    commander training program and, 97–99, 100

    defining characteristics, 99–100

    health effects of, 104–5

    interpersonal communication and, 101–4

    psychology-physiology connection and, 106–9

    workplace dynamics and, 99

Charities, 143

"Chasing a loss" behavior, 23–24

Chirac, Jacques, 160

Class rank, 71

Index

Cocaine, 140

Commander training program, 97–99, 100

Commitment to a held belief
  antidote to, 173–75
  Bush's experience, 37–38
  football strategy and, 29–30
  Homo erectus discovery and, 48
  Johnson's experience, 33–38
  KLM Flight 4805 crash and, 32–33
  loss aversion, combination with, 30–39
  optimism and, 37, 38
  twenty-dollar auction and, 30–32, 35, 188–89*n*

Community High School, 144–48

Conformity within groups, 153–57

Contextual model of diagnosis, 193*n*

Crew Resource Management (CRM) program, 163–68

Darwin, Charles, 45

Dawson, Charles, 52–55

Dees, Cathy, 166–67

Devil's advocate, 180

Diagnosis bias, 17
  antidotes to, 87–88, 177–78
  arbitrary information, reliance on, 91–94
  bipolar disorder epidemic and, 90–94, 96–97
  blinding effect of, 5–7, 74–75
  casual descriptions and, 73–74
  class rank and, 71
  contextual model of diagnosis and, 193*n*
  dismissal of facts, 79
  draft order as predictor of career trajectory and, 67–71, 75, 191*n*
  first impressions and, 77
  house purchases and, 79–80

ignoring objective data that contradicts initial diagnosis, 94–96
  irrelevant factors, focus on, 84–86
  job interviews and, 75–77, 80–84, 86, 87–88, 177
  marketing gimmicks and, 84–86
  meaning of, 70
  medical model of diagnosis and, 92–97
  "mirror, mirror" effect and, 86
  relationship longevity and, 77–79
  single word's power to alter perceptions, 71–73, 75
  value attribution and, 70, 74
  See also Chameleon effect

Diagnostic and Statistical Manual of Mental Disorders (DSM-III), 92–93, 94

Discounted prices, 57–59

Dissenter/blocker role in groups, 154–63, 167–68, 180

Draft order as predictor of career trajectory, 67–71, 75, 191*n*

Dubois, Eugene, 45–48, 50

Eden, Dov, 98

Egg sales, 17–18

Epting, Franz, 74–75, 100, 177, 178

Evolutionary theory, 43, 45, 48

Factor analysis, 191*n*

Fairness perception
  antidote to, 178–80
  behavior of others and, 118–19
  cultural differences in, 122–28, 129
  procedural justice and, 117–22, 128–29
  punishment of the undeserving and, 112–15, 117

Index

unfair deals rejected despite loss of profit, 115–17, 125–26

voicing of concerns and, 119–22

Falk, Dean, 42–44, 59, 60–63, 190*n*

Felons' perception of fairness, 119–21

Fernandez, Roberto, 3–4

Ferris Bueller's Day Off (film), 157–58

First impressions, 77

Flat-rate plans, 19–20

Football strategy, 27–30

Foucault, Jean-Pierre, 112, 115

France

   Iraq war, U.S.-French conflict regarding, 159–60

   perception of fairness in, 112–15, 117

Fund-raisers, 143

Fun-n-Gun football strategy, 28

Gibson, Elizabeth, 176

Golem effect, 100

Graduate Management Aptitude Test (GMAT) experiment, 136–39, 142

Great Society programs, 34, 36

Greenberg, Jack, 179

Group dynamics

   challenging authority, 166–67

   conformity within groups, 153–57

   dissenter/blocker role, 154–63, 167–68, 180

   initiator-blocker balance, 157–60

   KLM Flight 4805 crash and, 162–63

   observer role, 158–59, 165–66

   supporter role, 158

   in Supreme Court, 150–53, 154, 161, 162

   teamwork, culture of, 163–68

Grove, Andy, 174–75

Hamlin, David, 42–43, 59, 61

Handwerker, Nathan, 51–52

Hastings, Brian, 5–6

Healy, David, 93

Henrich, Joseph, 125–28

Hiring practices, 76–77, 88. *See also* Job interviews

Hoang, Ha, 68–69, 191*n*

Homo erectus, 46–48, 50, 54–55

Homo floresiensis, 42–44, 59–63, 190*n*

Hosking, Geoffrey, 123–25

House purchases, 79–80

Huffcutt, Allen, 75–77, 80, 81–83, 86, 87, 88, 192*n*

Incentives. *See* Motivation-reward relationship

Industrial safety practices, 168

Ingalls, Laura, 2

Initiator-blocker balance in groups, 157–60

Intel company, 174–75

Investing, 22–24, 173

Iraq war

   commitment to a held belief/loss aversion and, 37–38

   U.S.-French conflict regarding, 159–60

Irrational behavior, 3–7, 180–81

   psychological undercurrents and, 16–17

Island-effect phenomenon, 43, 59

Job interviews, 75–77, 80–84, 86, 87–88, 177

Johnson, Eric, 21

Johnson, Lyndon B., 33–38

Index

Joint responsibility, 124
Jordan, Michael, 67

Kahneman, Daniel, 38, 189*n*
Kanki, Barbara, 163–64
Kantor, David, 157
KLM Flight 4805 crash
  commitment to a held belief and,
    32–33
  group dynamics and, 162–63
  loss aversion and, 10–16, 21, 24
Knutson, Brian, 197*n*
Kraepelin, Emil, 92, 93

Label assignment. *See* Diagnosis
  bias
"Letting go of the past" strategy,
  173–75
Long-term planning, 171–73
Loss aversion, 17
  antidote to, 171–73
  Bush's experience, 37–38
  "chasing a loss" behavior,
    23–24
  commitment to a held belief,
    combination with, 30–39
  football strategy and, 27–29
  investing and, 22–24, 173
  Johnson's experience, 33–38
  KLM Flight 4805 crash and, 10–16,
    21, 24
  meaningfulness of potential loss
    and, 21–22
  optimism and, 37, 38
  pay-as-you-go vs. flat-rate plans,
    19–20
  price increases, overreaction to,
    18–19
  rental-car insurance and, 20–21
  twenty-dollar auction and, 30–32,
    35, 188–89*n*

MacDonald, Tara, 77–79
Machiguenga tribe, 126–28
Marketing gimmicks, 84–86
Medical model of diagnosis, 92–97
Medical safety practices, 167–68
"Mirror, mirror" effect, 86
Missing link, search for, 44–48, 54
Money-splitter experiment, 115–18,
  125–28
Moore, Gordon, 174–75
Morwood, Mike, 43, 44, 59
Motivation-reward relationship, 132
  addiction and, 140, 147, 148
  anticipation factor and, 148
  lowering standards to attain
    rewards, 144–48
  neurophysiology of, 139–44
  paradox of monetary rewards
    serving as disincentives,
    132–39
  pleasure-altruism conflict and,
    140–48

Nathan's Famous Hot Dogs, 51–52
NBA draft, 66–71
Neanderthals, 44–45
Neuroeconomics, 197*n*
Nuclear waste depositories, 132–35,
  141–42
Nucleus accumbens, 140

Observer role in groups, 158–59,
  165–66
Ohio State theater productions, 57–59
Olajuwon, Hakeem "The Dream,"
  66–67
Only the Paranoid Survive (Grove),
  174–75
Optimism, 37, 38
Orange juice sales, 19
Origin of Species (Darwin), 45

204

Index

Pay-as-you-go plans, 19–20

Personal construct theory, 177–78

Pharmaceutical industry, 93, 94

Pilot training, 163–67

Piltdown Man hoax, 52–55

Pleasure-altruism conflict, 140–48

Portland Trail Blazers, 66–67

Posterior superior temporal sulcus, 141

Price increases, overreaction to, 18–19

Procedural justice, 117–22, 128–29

Propositional thinking, 178

Psychology-physiology connection, 106–9

Psychotherapy, 94–96, 193n

Punishment of the undeserving, 112–15, 117

Putler, Daniel, 17–18

Pygmalion effect, 100

Rehnquist, William, 162

Relationship longevity, 77–79

Renshon, Jonathan, 189n

Rental-car insurance, 20–21

Rewards. *See* Motivation-reward relationship

Rip currents, 170–71

Roosevelt, Franklin D., 34

Ross, Mike, 77–79

Russia

  perception of fairness in, 123–25

  smiling practices in, 196–97n

Scalia, Antonin, 162

Selective serotonin reuptake inhibitors (SSRIs), 96–97, 193–94n

Shakespeare, William, 57

SoBe Adrenaline Rush experiment, 55–56, 175–76

Souvorov, Anton, 147

Space Shuttle *Challenger* disaster, 3–4

Spurrier, Steve, 27–28, 29, 30

Staw, Barry, 68–69, 191n

Stockton, John, 67

Suicide rates, 91, 96

Supporter role in groups, 158

Supreme Court, U.S., 150–53, 154, 161, 162

Swiss nuclear waste depositories, 132–35, 141–42

Tamayo, Rufino, 176–77

Teamwork, culture of, 163–68

Telephone conversations experiment, 101–4

Tres Personajes (Tamayo), 176–77

Tversky, Amos, 38

Twenty-dollar auction, 30–32, 35, 188–89n

University of Florida football program, 26–30

Value attribution, 17

  antidote to, 175–77

  Bell's violin playing and, 49–50, 57

  class rank and, 71

  diagnosis bias and, 70, 74

  discounted prices and, 57–59

  draft order as predictor of career trajectory and, 67–71, 75, 191n

  Homo erectus discovery and, 50, 54–55

  Homo floresiensis discovery and, 59, 62–63

  meaning of, 48–49

  Nathan's Famous Hot Dogs and, 51–52

  perceptions of subsequent information, impact on, 50–51, 55, 56

  Piltdown Man hoax and, 52–55

Index

SoBe Adrenaline Rush experiment
  and, 55–56, 175–76
Van Zanten, Jacob, 10–16, 21, 24,
  32–33, 162–63
Venture capitalists, 121–22
Vietnam War, 35–38
Villepin, Dominique de, 159–60

Walters, Jordan, 22–24, 171, 172, 173
Wampold, Bruce, 94–96, 99–100, 193*n*
Who Wants to Be a Millionaire (TV
  show)
  in France, 112–15, 117
  in Russia, 123–25
Workplace dynamics, 99

About the Authors

Ori Brafman is coauthor of *The Starfish and the Spider* and is a renowned organizational expert who regularly speaks before Fortune 500, governmental, and military audiences. A graduate of Stanford Business School, he lives in San Francisco.

Rom Brafman holds a Ph.D. in psychology and has taught university courses in personality and personal growth. His current research interests focus on the dynamics of interpersonal relationships. He has a private practice in Palo Alto, California.

Together they have been featured or quoted in many publications including the *Wall Street Journal*, *USA Today*, the *New York Times*, and the *Financial Times*, and have appeared on ABC News and NPR.